SO-APM-053

Anglo-Didáctica Linguistics Group

50
Tópicos en inglés sencillo y sus textos fonéticos

50
Topics in Easy English with Phonetic Transcription

ENGLISH LANGUAGE BOOKS

ANGLO DIDACTICA

ANGLO DIDACTICA PUBLISHING

Editorial Anglo Didáctica, S.L.
C/ Santiago de Compostela, 16
28034 Madrid – Spain.
Tel y fax: 91 378 01 88.

ISBN: 84-86623-84-7

Depósito legal: M. 31.240-2000

Imprenta Fareso, S. A.
Paseo de la Dirección, 5
28039 Madrid

Impreso en España.
Printed in Spain.

Phonetic Symbols

Vowels

i: eat /i:t/
ɪ it /ɪt/
e let /let/
æ back /bæk/
ɑ: car /kɑ:/
ɒ hot /hɒt/
ɔ: horse /hɔ:s/
ʊ book /bʊk/
u: food /fu:d/
ʌ but /bʌt/
ɜ: sir /sɜ:/
ə a /ə/

Dipthongs

eɪ make /meɪk/
əʊ road /rəʊd/
aɪ eye /aɪ/
aʊ cow /kaʊ/
ɔɪ toy /tɔɪ/
ɪə here /hɪə/
eə hair /heə/
ʊə poor /pʊə/

Consonants

p pipe /paɪp/
b book /bʊk/
t time /taɪm/
d day /deɪ/
k cake /keɪk/
g girl /gɜ:l/
f fine /faɪn/
v very /'verɪ/
θ think /θɪŋk/
ð this /ðɪs/
s sea /si:/
z please /pli:z/
ʃ shoe /ʃu:/
ʒ pleasure /'pleʒə/
tʃ church /tʃɜ:tʃ/
dʒ just /dʒʌst/
m man /mæn/
n none /nʌn/
ŋ thing /θɪŋ/
r right /raɪt/
h hurry /'hʌrɪ/
l tell /tel/
w well /wel/
j yes /jes/

En la transcripción de los textos se ha incluido el acento secundario (situado abajo (,) por ejemplo 'træfɪk ˌlaɪts) para indicar aquellas sílabas o palabras que llevan un acento menos fuerte que el principal (situado arriba (') por ejemplo 'træfɪk ˌlaɪts) El acento secundario tiene por objeto reforzar dichas sílabas o palabras que quedan en posición inacentuada.

Hay que tener en cuenta que tanto la transcripción fonética de los textos como la distribución de los acentos en las palabras obedecen a un criterio "standard."

Para las distintas variantes que existen en la transcripción de las palabras consúltese la obra *English Pronouncing Dictionary* del autor *Daniel Jones - Cambridge University Press*.

Como complemento de este libro, se sugiere consultar los títulos: *La pronunciación inglesa. Fonética y fonología, Fonética funcional inglesa, Práctica de pronunciación inglesa*, publicados por *Anglo Didáctica, S.L.*

1
AGE

The teacher is asking questions in class. First, he asks Tony, a boy in the second row.

- Tony, how old are you?
- I'm thirteen years old.
- How old is your brother Robert?
- He's fourteen.
- So, Robert is one year older than you, and you are one year younger than Robert.

Then the teacher asks Betty, a girl in the third row.

- Betty, how many brothers or sisters have you got?
- I have two brothers and one sister.
- Who's the eldest?
- My sister Jean is the eldest. She's twenty-two.
- Who's the youngest?
- My brother Bruce is the youngest. He's only five and a half.

At this moment, the bell rings and all the children go out into the playground.

age edad
bell campana, timbre
boy muchacho
brother hermano
children niños
the eldest el mayor

girl muchacha
half medio
older mayor
only solamente
playground patio de recreo

row fila
sister hermana
teacher profesor
year año
younger menor
the youngest el menor

How old are you? ¿Qué edad tienes?
I'm thirteen years old Tengo trece años.

4

1
'eɪdʒ

ðə 'ti:tʃər ɪz 'ɑ:skɪŋ 'kwestʃənz ɪn 'klɑ:s. 'fɜ:st, hɪ 'ɑ:sks 'təʊnɪ, ə 'bɔɪ ɪn ðə 'sekənd 'rəʊ.

- 'təʊnɪ, haʊ 'əʊld ə jʊ?
- aɪm 'θɜ:ti:n 'jɪəz 'əʊld.
- haʊ 'əʊld ɪz jɔ: 'brʌðə 'rɒbət?
- hi:z 'fɔ:'ti:n.
- səʊ, 'rɒbət ɪz 'wʌn 'jɪər 'əʊldə ðən 'ju:, ən jʊ ə 'wʌn 'jɪə 'jʌŋgə ðən 'rɒbət.

ðen ðə 'ti:tʃə 'ɑ:sks 'betɪ, ə 'gɜ:l ɪn ðə 'θɜ:d 'rəʊ.

- 'betɪ, 'haʊ menɪ 'brʌðəz ɔ: 'sɪstəz həv jʊ 'gɒt?
- aɪ hæv 'tu: 'brʌðəz ən 'wʌn 'sɪstə.
- 'hu:z ɪz ðɪ 'eldɪst?
- maɪ 'sɪstə 'dʒi:n ɪz ðɪ 'eldɪst. ʃi:z ˌtwentɪ 'tu:
- 'hu:z ɪz ðə 'jʌŋgɪst?
- maɪ 'brʌðə 'bru:s ɪz ðə 'jʌŋgɪst. hi:z 'əʊnlɪ 'faɪv ənd ə 'hɑ:f.

ət ðɪs 'məʊmənt, ðə 'bel 'rɪŋz ənd 'ɔ:l ðə 'tʃɪldrən gəʊ 'aʊt ɪntə ðə 'pleɪgraʊnd.

2
ASKING THE WAY

When you are in a town you do not know very well, you can easily get lost. If you ever lose your way in a town in Great Britain, remember this conversation between a foreigner and a policeman:

- Can you tell me the way to the Alexandra Hotel, please?
- It's a bit awkward to direct you from here. Let me see... Turn left at this corner and walk down until you come to the traffic lights. Take the second street on the right and continue until you reach a big square. Go straight on for about three hundred yards, and you will see the Alexandra Hotel opposite a very big church.
- Is it very far?
- Well, it's quite a long way.
- I'm a stranger here and I don't know this town. I'm afraid I may get lost.
- Well, you can also catch a number twenty bus at that bus stop over there. Get off at Penbroke Square and then you can walk to the hotel.
- Thank you very much. I'll do that. Goodbye.
- Not at all. Goodbye.

awkward difícil	left izquierda	square plaza
church iglesia	lose perder	stranger forastero
corner esquina	opposite enfrente de	street calle
foreigner extranjero	policeman guardia	town ciudad
get lost perderse	reach llegar a	way camino
get off apearse	right derecha	yard yarda

Can you tell me the way to ... ? ¿Puede decirme cómo se va a ...?
Go straight on Siga derecho.
Is it very far? ¿Está muy lejos?
It's quite a long way Está bastante lejos.

6

2
'ɑ:skɪŋ ðə 'weɪ

wen ju ər ɪn ə 'taʊn ju du 'nɒt 'nəʊ verɪ 'wel, ju kən 'i:zɪlɪ
get 'lɒst. ɪf ju 'evə 'lu:z jɔ: 'weɪ ɪn ə 'taʊn ɪn 'greɪt 'brɪtən,
rɪ'membə ðɪs ˌkɒnvə'seɪʃən bɪtwi:n ə 'fɒrɪnə ənd ə pə'li:smən :

- kən ju 'tel mɪ ðə 'weɪ tə ði ˌælɪg'zændrə həʊ'tel, 'pli:z?
- ɪts ə 'bɪt 'ɔ:kwəd tə dɪ'rekt ju frəm 'hɪə. 'let mɪ 'si: ...
  'tɜ:n 'left ət ðɪs 'kɔ:nə ən 'wɔ:k 'daʊn ʌntɪl ju 'kʌm tə
  ðə 'træfɪk ˌlaɪts. 'teɪk ðə 'sekənd 'stri:t ɒn ðə 'raɪt ən
  kən'tɪnju: ʌntɪl ju 'ri:tʃ ə 'bɪg 'skweə. 'gəʊ 'streɪt 'ɒn fər
  əbaʊt 'θri: hʌndrɪd 'jɑ:dz, ən ju wɪl 'si: ði ˌælɪg'zændrə
  həʊ'tel 'ɒpəzɪt ə 'verɪ bɪg 'tʃɜ:tʃ.
- ɪz ɪt 'verɪ 'fɑ:?
- 'wel, ɪts 'kwaɪt ə lɒŋ 'weɪ.
- aɪm ə 'streɪndʒə 'hɪə ənd aɪ 'dəʊn 'nəʊ ðɪs 'taʊn. aɪm
  ə'freɪd aɪ meɪ 'get 'lɒst.
- 'wel, ju kən 'ɔ:lsəʊ 'kætʃ ə 'nʌmbə 'twentɪ 'bʌs ət ðæt
  'bʌs stɒp əʊvə 'ðeə. 'get 'ɒf ət 'penbrəʊk 'skweə ən ðen
  ju kən 'wɔ:k tə ðə həʊ'tel.
- 'θæŋk ju 'verɪ 'mʌtʃ. aɪl 'du: 'ðæt. gʊd'baɪ.
- 'nɒt ət 'ɔ:l. gʊd'baɪ.

3

AT THE BANK

A bank is a place where you keep your money, and where you can cash cheques. Here is a conversation between a tourist and a bank clerk:

- Good morning. Can I cash traveller's cheques here?
- Yes. How much do you want to change?
- A hundred pounds.
- May I have your passport? Thank you. How would you like it? In five-pound notes?
- Yes, please.
- Here you are.
- Thank you. I have some Spanish money with me. Can I change it into English currency?
- Yes, of course.
- What's the rate today?
- About 250 pesetas to the pound. How many pesetas would you like to change?
- 5,000 pesetas.
- Just a moment, please.

The clerk takes the Spanish money, goes away and comes back a moment later with a piece of paper in one hand and some English money in the other.

- Here you are. Twenty pounds. Will you sign here, please?
- Yes. Thank you very much. Goodbye.
- Goodbye.

cash cobrar	**coin** moneda	**note** billete
change cambiar	**currency** moneda	**rate** cambio
clerk empleado	**money** dinero	**traveller** viajero

3

ət ðə 'bæŋk

ə 'bæŋk ɪz ə 'pleɪs weə ju 'ki:p jɔ: 'mʌnɪ, ən weə ju kən 'kæʃ 'tʃeks. 'hɪər ɪz ə ˌkɒnvə'seɪʃən bɪtwi:n ə 'tuərɪst ənd ə 'bæŋk klɑ:k :-

- gʊd'mɔ:nɪŋ, kən aɪ 'kæʃ 'trævələz ˌtʃeks 'hɪə?
- 'jes. 'haʊ 'mʌtʃ dʊ ju 'wɒnt tə 'tʃeɪndʒ?
- ə 'hʌndrɪd 'paʊndz.
- meɪ aɪ hæv jɔ: 'pɑ:spɔ:t? 'θæŋk ju. 'haʊ wəd ju 'laɪk ɪt? ɪn 'faɪv paʊnd 'nəʊts?
- 'jes, 'pli:z.
- 'hɪə ju 'ɑ:
- 'θæŋk ju. aɪ hæv səm 'spænɪʃ·'mʌnɪ wɪð mɪ. kən aɪ 'tʃeɪndʒ ɪt ɪntʊ 'ɪŋglɪʃ 'kʌrənsɪ?
- 'jes, əv 'kɔ:s.
- 'wɒts ðə 'reɪt tə'deɪ?
- əbaʊt 'tu: hʌndrɪd ən 'fɪftɪ pə'seɪtəz tə ðə 'paʊnd. 'haʊ menɪ pə'seɪtəz wəd ju 'laɪk tə 'tʃeɪndʒ?
- 'faɪv θaʊzənd pə'seɪtəz.
- 'dʒʌst ə 'məʊmənt, 'pli:z.

ðə 'klɑ:k 'teɪks ðə 'spænɪʃ 'mʌnɪ, 'gəʊz ə'weɪ ən 'kʌmz 'bæk ə 'məʊmənt 'leɪtə wɪð ə 'pi:s əv 'peɪpə ɪn 'wʌn 'hænd ən səm 'ɪŋglɪʃ 'mʌnɪ ɪn ðɪ 'ʌðə.

- 'hɪə ju 'ɑ: - 'twentɪ 'paʊndz. wɪl ju 'saɪn 'hɪə, 'pli:z?
- 'jes. 'θæŋk ju verɪ 'mʌtʃ. gʊd'baɪ.
- gʊd'baɪ.

4

A BIRTHDAY

Today is Henry's birthday. He is having a party. Mrs Alison, Henry's mother, is getting everything ready for the party. She is now making cheese sandwiches and ham sandwiches. There is a big table in the middle of the sitting-room, where there are a lot of drinks, such as coke, lemonade and tomato juice.

Mr Alison, Henry's father, is not at home now. He has gone to the nearest cake shop to buy a cake with six candles, for Henry is six years old today.

At about three, the doorbell begins to ring. Henry's friends are coming to the party. Each of his friends brings him a present. When they come into the sitting-room, they say to Henry, "Many happy returns of the day!" Then they all begin to eat and drink.

At about four, Mr Alison comes home with the cake. He puts it on the table, lights the candles and asks Henry to blow them out. At that moment everybody sings:

> Happy birthday to you!
> Happy birthday to you!
> Happy birthday, dear Henry!
> Happy birthday to you!

blow out apagar	**friends** amigos	**party** fiesta
cake tarta	**happy** feliz	**present** regalo
candles velas	**light** encender	**sing** cantar

Many happy returns of the day Que cumplas muchos más.

10

4

ə ˈbɜːθdeɪ

təˈdeɪ ɪz ˈhenrɪz ˈbɜːθdeɪ. hɪ ɪz hævɪŋ ə ˈpɑːtɪ. mɪsɪz ˈælɪsən, ˈhenrɪz ˈmʌðə, ɪz ˈgetɪŋ ˈevrɪθɪŋ ˈredɪ fə ðə ˈpɑːtɪ. ʃɪ ɪz ˈnaʊ ˈmeɪkɪŋ ˈtʃiːz ˈsænwɪdʒɪz ən ˈhæm sænwɪdʒɪz. ðər ɪz ə ˈbɪg ˈteɪbl ɪn ðə ˈmɪdl əv ðə ˈsɪtɪŋˌrʊm, weə ðər ər ə ˈlɒt əv ˈdrɪŋks, sʌtʃ əz ˈkəʊk, ˌlemənˈeɪd ən təˈmɑːtəʊ ˌdʒuːs.

mɪstər ˈælɪsən, ˈhenrɪz ˈfɑːðə, ɪz ˈnɒt ət ˈhəʊm ˈnaʊ. hɪ həz ˈgɒn tə ðə ˈnɪərɪst ˈkeɪk ʃɒp tə ˈbaɪ ə ˈkeɪk wɪð ˈsɪks ˈkændlz, fɔː ˈhenrɪ ɪz ˈsɪks ˈjɪəz ˈəʊld təˈdeɪ.

ət əbaʊt ˈθriː, ðə ˈdɔːbel brˈgɪnz tə ˈrɪŋ. ˈhenrɪz ˈfrendz ə ˈkʌmɪŋ tə ðə ˈpɑːtɪ. ˈiːtʃ əv hɪz ˈfrendz ˈbrɪŋz hɪm ə ˈprezənt. wen ðeɪ ˈkʌm ɪntə ðə ˈsɪtɪŋˌrʊm, ðeɪ ˈseɪ tə ˈhenrɪ, ˈmenɪ ˈhæpɪ rɪˈtɜːnz əv ðə ˈdeɪ! ðen ðeɪ ˈɔːl brˈgɪn tʊ ˈiːt ən ˈdrɪŋk.

ət əbaʊt ˈfɔː, mɪstər ˈælɪsən ˈkʌmz ˈhəʊm wɪð ðə ˈkeɪk. hɪ ˈpʊts ɪt ɒn ðə ˈteɪbl, ˈlaɪts ðə ˈkændlz ən ˈɑːsks ˈhenrɪ tə ˈbləʊ ðəm ˈaʊt. ət ðæt ˈməʊmənt ˈevrɪˌbɒdɪ ˈsɪŋz :-

ˈhæpɪ ˈbɜːθdeɪ tʊ ˈjuː!
ˈhæpɪ ˈbɜːθdeɪ tʊ ˈjuː!
ˈhæpɪ ˈbɜːθdeɪ, ˈdɪə ˈhenrɪ!
ˈhæpɪ ˈbɜːθdeɪ tʊ ˈjuː!

5
THE CALENDAR

When we want to see the date, we look at the calendar.

There are seven days in a week, four weeks in a month, and twelve months in a year. There are 365 days in a year. Let's have a look at the calendar:

- What day is it today?
- Today is Monday.
- What day was it yesterday?
- Yesterday was Sunday.
- What day is it tomorrow?
- Tomorrow is Tuesday.

- What's the date today?
- It's the tenth of April, nineteen ninety-nine.
- What was the date yesterday?
- It was the ninth of April, nineteen ninety-nine.
- What's the date tomorrow?
- It's the eleventh of April, nineteen ninety-nine.

****

- Yesterday was Sunday, the ninth of April, nineteen ninety-nine.
- Today is Monday, the tenth of April, nineteen ninety-nine.
- Tomorrow is Tuesday, the eleventh of April, nineteen ninety-nine.

calendar calendario
date fecha
day día

look at mirar
month mes
today hoy

tomorrow mañana
week semana
yesterday ayer

Let's have a look Miremos.

5
ðə ˈkælɪndə

wen wɪ ˈwɒnt tə ˈsi: ðə ˈdeɪt, wɪ ˈlʊk ət ðə ˈkælɪndə.
ðər ə ˈsevən ˈdeɪz ɪn ə ˈwi:k, ˈfɔ: ˈwi:ks ɪn ə ˈmʌnθ, ən
ˈtwelv ˈmʌnθs ɪn ə ˈjɪə. ðər ə ˈθri: hʌndrɪd ən ˈsɪkstɪ faɪv
ˈdeɪz ɪn ə ˈjɪə. ˈlets hæv ə ˈlʊk ət ðə ˈkælɪndə :-

- wɒt ˈdeɪ ɪz ɪt təˈdeɪ?
- təˈdeɪ ɪz ˈmʌndɪ.
- wɒt ˈdeɪ wəz ɪt ˈjestədɪ?
- ˈjestədɪ wəz ˈsʌndɪ.
- wɒt ˈdeɪ ɪz ɪt təˈmɒrəʊ?
- təˈmɒrəʊ ɪz ˈtju:zdɪ.

- ˈwɒts ðə ˈdeɪt təˈdeɪ?
- ɪts ðə ˈtenθ əv ˈeɪprəl, ˈnaɪnti:n ˌnaɪntɪ ˈnaɪn.
- ˈwɒt wəz ðə ˈdeɪt ˈjestədɪ?
- ɪt wəz ðə ˈnaɪnθ əv ˈeɪprəl, ˈnaɪnti:n ˌnaɪntɪ ˈnaɪn.
- ˈwɒts ðə ˈdeɪt təˈmɒrəʊ?
- ɪts ðɪ ɪˈlevənθ əv ˈeɪprəl, ˈnaɪnti:n ˌnaɪntɪ ˈnaɪn.

- ˈjestədɪ wəz ˈsʌndɪ, ðə ˈnaɪnθ əv ˈeɪprəl, ˈnaɪnti:n ˌnaɪntɪ
  ˈnaɪn.
- təˈdeɪ ɪz ˈmʌndɪ, ðə ˈtenθ əv ˈeɪprəl, ˈnaɪnti:n ˌnaɪntɪ ˈnaɪn.
- təˈmɒrəʊ ɪz ˈtju:zdɪ, ðɪ ɪˈlevənθ əv ˈeɪprəl, ˈnaɪnti:n ˌnaɪntɪ
  ˈnaɪn.

6

CAR MAINTENANCE

- Can you have a look at my car? It isn't going very well.
- What's the matter with it?
- There must be something wrong with the carburettor. I think it needs readjusting.
- Let me see... Yes, I think it's the carburettor. We shall have to dismantle it.
- Will you need to dismantle the whole engine?
- No, just the carburettor. Look, the battery needs recharging, and look at this tyre. It's almost flat. We shall have to change it.

Then the mechanic calls a boy and says to him:

- Get the jack and lift the car.

When the car has been lifted, the boy takes off the wheel and puts on the spare one.

- There's a puncture. Look.
- I would like you to have a look at the brakes. I think that the foot-brake is all right, but the hand-brake is rather loose.
- What about the steering? Is it all right?
- There's something wrong with it, but I don't know what.
- When will the car be ready?
- Come back tomorrow morning and it will be ready then.

battery batería	**jack** gato	**spare** de repuesto
brakes frenos	**lift** levantar	**steering** dirección
car coche	**loose** flojo	**take off** quitar
engine motor	**puncture** pinchazo	**tyre** neumático
flat pinchada	**ready** listo	**wheel** rueda

14

6
'kɑː meɪntənəns

- kən jʊ hæv ə 'lʊk ət maɪ 'kɑː? ɪt 'ɪzənt 'gəʊɪŋ verɪ 'wel.
- 'wɒts ðə 'mætə wɪð ɪt?
- ðeə mʌst bɪ 'sʌmθɪŋ 'rɒŋ wɪð ðə ˌkɑːbjʊ'retə. aɪ 'θɪŋk ɪt 'niːdz ˌriːə'dʒʌstɪŋ.
- 'let mɪ 'siː ... 'jes, aɪ 'θɪŋk ɪts ðə ˌkɑːbjʊ'retə. wi ʃəl 'hæv tə dɪs'mæntl ɪt.
- wɪl jʊ 'niːd tə dɪs'mæntl ðə 'həʊl 'endʒɪn?
- 'nəʊ, 'dʒʌst ðə ˌkɑːbjʊ'retə. 'lʊk, ðə 'bætərɪ 'niːdz ˌriːt'ʃɑːdʒɪŋ, ən 'lʊk ət ðɪs 'taɪə. ɪts 'ɔːlməʊst 'flæt. wi ʃəl 'hæv tə 'tʃeɪndʒ ɪt.

ðen ðə mɪ'kænɪk 'kɔːlz ə 'bɔɪ ən 'sez tə hɪm :-

- 'get ðə 'dʒæk ən 'lɪft ðə 'kɑː

wen ðə 'kɑː həz bɪn 'lɪftɪd, ðə 'bɔɪ 'teɪks ɒf ðə 'wiːl ən 'pʊts ɒn ðə 'speə wʌn.

- ðəz ə 'pʌŋktʃə. 'lʊk.
- aɪ wəd 'laɪk jʊ tə hæv ə 'lʊk ət ðə 'breɪks. aɪ 'θɪŋk ðət ðə 'fʊtbreɪk ɪz ɔːl 'raɪt, bət ðə 'hændbreɪk ɪz 'rɑːðə 'luːs.
- 'wɒt əbaʊt ðə 'stɪərɪŋ? ɪz ɪt ɔːl 'raɪt?
- ðəz 'sʌmθɪŋ 'rɒŋ wɪð ɪt, bət aɪ 'dəʊn nəʊ 'wɒt.
- 'wen wɪl ðə 'kɑː bɪ 'redɪ?
- 'kʌm 'bæk tə'mɒrəʊ 'mɔːnɪŋ ənd ɪt wɪl bɪ 'redɪ ðen.

7
CATCHING A TRAIN

- Where's the booking office, please?
- It's over there.
- Thank you.
- One first class return to Oxford, please.
- Here you are.
- How much is it?
- 8 pounds.
- Thank you.
- Which platform for the Oxford train, please?
- Platform three, through the subway.
- What time does the train go?
- It goes at five o'clock. In ten minutes' time.
- Thank you.

A few minutes later, the train arrives.

- Is this the train to Oxford?
- Yes, it is.
- May I put my case on the rack?
- Certainly, I'll help you.
- Thank you.
- What time does this train get to Oxford?
- At about six.

Then the passenger who has just come into the compartment takes out a magazine and begins to read.

case maleta	**passenger** pasajero	**rack** rejilla
later más tarde	**platform** andén	**through** a través de

One first class return to Oxford. Un billete de primera clase de ida y vuelta a Oxford.

7
'kætʃɪŋ ə 'treɪn

- 'weəz ðə 'bʊkɪŋ ˌɒfɪs, 'pliːz?
- ɪts 'əʊvə 'ðeə.
- 'θæŋk jʊ.
- 'wʌn 'fɜːst 'klɑːs rɪ'tɜːn tʊ 'ɒksfəd, 'pliːz.
- 'hɪə jʊ 'ɑː
- 'haʊ 'mʌtʃ ɪz ɪt?
- 'eɪt 'paʊndz.
- 'θæŋk jʊ.
- wɪtʃ 'plætfɔːm fə ðɪ 'ɒksfəd 'treɪn, 'pliːz?
- 'plætfɔːm 'θriː, θruː ðə 'sʌbweɪ.
- wɒt 'taɪm dəz ðə 'treɪn 'gəʊ?
- ɪt gəʊz ət 'faɪv əklɒk. ɪn 'ten mɪnɪts 'taɪm.
- 'θæŋk jʊ.

ə 'fjuː mɪnɪts 'leɪtə, ðə 'treɪn ə'raɪvz.

- ɪz 'ðɪs ðə 'treɪn tʊ 'ɒksfəd?
- 'jes, ɪt 'ɪz.
- meɪ aɪ 'pʊt maɪ 'keɪs ɒn ðə 'ræk?
- 'sɜːtənlɪ. aɪl 'help jʊ.
- 'θæŋk jʊ.
- wɒt 'taɪm dəz ðɪs 'treɪn 'get tʊ 'ɒksfəd?
- ət əbaʊt 'sɪks.

ðen ðə 'pæsɪndʒə hʊ həz 'dʒʌst 'kʌm ɪntə ðə kəm'pɑːtmənt 'teɪks aʊt ə ˌmægə'ziːn ən bɪ'gɪnz tə 'riːd.

8
AT THE CINEMA

Albert meets Jack in the street.
- Where are you going, Jack?
- I'm going to the cinema.
- What film are you going to see?
- I'm going to see a western. I like westerns very much. Do you want to come with me?
- What film is it?
- "Smoking Guns."
- Who's in it?
- Anthony Kelly and Betty Oliver.
- It must be a good film. I'll come with you as I'm free this afternoon. Where are they showing it?
- At the Alhambra.
- How shall we go?
- We'll catch a number 20 bus.

****

- Here we are. The cinema is over there.
- Here's the box office. Shall we go downstairs?
- Let's go upstairs. It's cheaper.
- Let's go in now.
- Here's the usherette. She's pointing the torch at us.
- Let me see. Row G. There are two seats there.
- This is too near the screen.
- Well, you can sit down there, in row K, if you like.
- Yes, that's much better. Thank you.

box office taquilla	**row** fila	**show** proyectar
downstairs abajo	**screen** pantalla	**upstairs** arriba
torch linterna	**seat** asiento	**usherette** acomodadora

8
ət ðə 'sɪnəmə

'ælbət 'mi:ts 'dʒæk ɪn ðə 'stri:t.
- 'weər ə ju 'gəʊɪŋ, 'dʒæk?
- aɪm gəʊɪŋ tə ðə 'sɪnəmə.
- wɒt 'fɪlm ə ju 'gəʊɪŋ tə 'si:?
- aɪm 'gəʊɪŋ tə si: ə 'westən. aɪ 'laɪk 'westənz verɪ 'mʌtʃ.
  du ju 'wɒnt tə 'kʌm wɪð mɪ?
- wɒt 'fɪlm ɪz ɪt?
- 'sməʊkɪŋ 'gʌnz.
- 'hu:z ɪn ɪt?
- 'æntənɪ 'kelɪ ən 'betɪ 'ɒlɪvə.
- ɪt mʌst bɪ ə 'gʊd 'fɪlm. aɪl 'kʌm wɪð ju əz aɪm 'fri: ðɪs
  ˌɑ:ftə'nu:n.
- 'weər ə ðeɪ 'ʃəʊɪŋ ɪt?
- ət ðɪ æl'hæmbrə.
- 'haʊ ʃəl wɪ 'gəʊ?
- wi:l 'kætʃ ə 'nʌmbə 'twentɪ 'bʌs.
                    ****
- 'hɪə wɪ 'ɑ: - ðə 'sɪnəmə ɪz 'əʊvə 'ðeə.
- 'hɪəz ðə 'bʊks ɒfɪs. ʃəl wɪ 'gəʊ daʊn'steəz?
- 'lets gəʊ 'ʌpsteəz. ɪts 'tʃi:pə.
- 'lets 'gəʊ 'ɪn 'naʊ.
- 'hɪəz ðɪ ʌʃə'ret. ʃi:z 'pɔɪntɪŋ ðə 'tɔ:tʃ ət əs.
- 'let mɪ 'si: - 'rəʊ 'dʒi: - ðər ə 'tu: 'si:ts 'ðeə.
- 'ðɪs ɪz 'tu: 'nɪə ðə 'skri:n.
- 'wel, ju kən 'sɪt 'daʊn 'ðeə, ɪn 'rəʊ 'keɪ, ɪf ju 'laɪk.
- 'jes, 'ðæts mʌtʃ 'betə. 'θæŋk ju.

19

9
CLOTHES

There are men's clothes and women's clothes.

We put on our clothes when we get up and take them off when we go to bed.

In winter we wear heavy or thick clothes because it is cold. In summer we wear light or thin clothes because it is hot.

The clothes men wear are the following: shirt, pullover, trousers, jacket, suit, hat, shoes, overcoat and raincoat.

The clothes women wear are the following: blouse, cardigan, dress, skirt, shoes, slacks, hat and coat.

Underclothes are: for men, vest, underpants and socks. For women, panties, bra and stockings or tights.

To go to a party in the evening, a man wears a dinner jacket, and a woman wears an evening dress.

When we are at home, before going to bed, or when we get up, we wear a dressing gown.

When we are in bed, we wear pyjamas. Some women wear a night-dress in bed.

bed cama	**night-dress** camisón	**stockings** medias
blouse blusa	**overcoat** abrigo	**take off** quitarse
bra sujetador	**panties** bragas	**thin** delgado
cardigan rebeca	**put on** ponerse	**tights** leotardos, pantys
clothes ropa	**raincoat** gabardina	**underclothes** ropa
coat abrigo	**shirt** camisa	interior
dress vestido	**skirt** falda	**underpants** calzoncillos
dressing gown bata	**slacks** pantalones	**vest** camiseta
hat sombrero	**socks** calcetines	**wear** llevar puesto

9
'kləʊðz

ðər ə 'menz 'kləʊðz ən 'wimɪnz kləʊðz.

wɪ 'pʊt ɒn aʊə 'kləʊðz wen wɪ 'get 'ʌp ən 'teɪk ðəm 'ɒf wen wɪ 'gəʊ tə 'bed.

ɪn 'wɪntə wɪ 'weə 'hevɪ ɔ: 'θɪk 'kləʊðz bɪkɒz ɪt ɪz 'kəʊld.

ɪn 'sʌmə wɪ 'weə 'laɪt ɔ: 'θɪn kləʊðz bɪkɒz ɪt ɪz 'hɒt.

ðə 'kləʊðz 'men 'weər ə ðə 'fɒləʊɪŋ - 'ʃɜ:t, 'pʊləʊvə, 'traʊzəz, 'dʒækɪt, 'su:t, 'hæt, 'ʃu:z, 'əʊvəkəʊt ən 'reɪnkəʊt.

ðə 'kləʊðz 'wimɪn 'weər ə ðə 'fɒləʊɪŋ - 'blaʊz, 'ka:dɪgən, 'dres, 'skɜ:t, 'ʃu:z, 'slæks, 'hæt ən 'kəʊt.

'ʌndəkləʊðz 'a: - fə 'men, 'vest, 'ʌndəpænts ən 'sɒks.

fə 'wimɪn, 'pæntɪz, 'bra: ən 'stɒkɪŋz ɔ: 'taɪts.

tə 'gəʊ tʊ ə 'pa:tɪ ɪn ðɪ 'i:vnɪŋ, ə 'mæn 'weəz ə 'dɪnə ˌdʒækɪt, ən ə 'wʊmən 'weəz ən 'i:vnɪŋ ˌdres.

wen wɪ ər ət 'həʊm, bɪfɔ: 'gəʊɪŋ tə 'bed, ɔ: wen wɪ 'get 'ʌp, wɪ 'weər ə 'dresɪŋ ˌgaʊn.

wen wɪ ər ɪn 'bed, wɪ 'weə pɪ'dʒa:məz. 'sʌm 'wimɪn 'weər ə 'naɪtdres ɪn 'bed.

10
COLOURS

Blue, green, red, yellow, brown, black, white, grey and pink are colours.

The sky is blue. The grass is green. Blood is red. A banana is yellow. Earth is brown. Coal is black. The snow is white. An elephant is grey. Pink is a pale red colour. Roses may be pink or red.

Orange is a mixture of red and yellow. Purple or violet is a mixture of red and blue. Some colours may be lightened or darkened by adding white or black. So we can say: light brown, dark brown; light green, dark green; light blue, dark blue. Grey is a colour between black and white. The sky is blue, but it can be grey on a cloudy day.

When we want to say that something is rather green, but not exactly green, we say "it is greenish". In the same way, we can say "greyish", "bluish", "whitish", etc.

Can you answer these questions?

- What colour is the Spanish flag?
- What colour is the French flag?
- What colour is the Italian flag?
- What colour is the German flag?
- What colour is the British flag?

black negro
blood sangre
blue azul
bluish azulado
brown marrón
colour color
dark oscuro
darkened oscurecido

flag bandera
green verde
greenish verdoso
grey gris
greyish grisáceo
light claro
lightened aclarado
mixture mezcla

pale pálido
purple morado
rather bastante
red rojo
violet violeta
white blanco
whitish blanquecino
yellow amarillo

22

10
'kʌləz

'blu:, 'gri:n, 'red, 'jeləu, 'braun, 'blæk, 'waɪt, 'greɪ ən
'pɪŋk ə 'kʌləz.

ðə 'skaɪ ɪz 'blu:. ðə 'gra:s ɪz 'gri:n. 'blʌd ɪz 'red. ə
bə'na:nə ɪz 'jeləu. 'ɜ:θ ɪz 'braun. 'kəul ɪz 'blæk. ðə 'snəu
ɪz 'waɪt. ən 'elɪfənt ɪz 'greɪ. 'pɪŋk ɪz ə 'peɪl red 'kʌlə. 'rəuzɪz
meɪ bɪ 'pɪŋk ɔ: 'red.

'ɒrɪndʒ ɪz ə 'mɪkstʃər əv 'red ən 'jeləu. 'pɜ:pl ɔ: 'vaɪəlɪt ɪz
ə 'mɪkstʃər əv 'red ən 'blu: 'sʌm 'kʌləz meɪ bɪ 'laɪtənd ɔ:
'da:kənd baɪ 'ædɪŋ 'waɪt ɔ: 'blæk. səu wɪ kən 'seɪ - 'laɪt
'braun, 'da:k 'braun, 'laɪt 'gri:n, 'da:k 'gri:n, 'laɪt 'blu:, 'da:k
'blu: 'greɪ ɪz ə 'kʌlə bɪtwi:n 'blæk ən 'waɪt. ðə 'skaɪ ɪz
'blu:, bət ɪt kən bɪ 'greɪ ɒn ə 'klaudɪ 'deɪ.

wen wɪ 'wɒnt tə 'seɪ ðət 'sʌmθɪŋ ɪz 'ra:ðə 'gri:n, bət 'nɒt
ɪg'zæktlɪ gri:n, wɪ seɪ ɪt ɪz 'gri:nɪʃ. ɪn ðə 'seɪm 'weɪ, wɪ
kən 'seɪ 'greɪɪʃ, 'blu:ɪʃ, 'waɪtɪʃ, ɪt'setrə.

kən ju 'a:nsə ði:z 'kwestʃənz?

- wɒt 'kʌlər ɪz ðə 'spænɪʃ 'flæg?
- wɒt 'kʌlər ɪz ðə 'frentʃ 'flæg?
- wɒt 'kʌlər ɪz ðɪ ɪ'tæljən 'flæg?
- wɒt 'kʌlər ɪz ðə 'dʒɜ:mən 'flæg?
- wɒt 'kʌlər ɪz ðə 'brɪtɪʃ 'flæg?

11
COUNTRIES AND LANGUAGES

In Europe there are many countries. Those which are nearest to Spain are Portugal, France, Italy, and Great Britain. They speak Portuguese in Portugal, French in France, Italian in Italy, and English in Great Britain.

In Spain there are a lot of tourists in summer. They come from different countries, especially from France, Germany and Great Britain. They come to visit Spain.

Here is a conversation between a Spaniard and some foreign tourists:

****

- What's your name?
- My name's Robert.
- Where do you come from?
- I come from England. I'm English. I speak English.

****

- What's your name?
- My name's Jacques.
- Where were you born?
- I was born in France. I'm French. I speak French.

countries países	**Germany** Alemania	**Portuguese** portugués
England Inglaterra	**Italian** italiano	**Spain** España
Europe Europa	**Italy** Italia	**Spaniard** español
foreign extranjero	**languages** idiomas	**Spanish** español
France Francia	**many** muchos	**speak** hablar
French francés	**nearest** más cerca	**summer** verano

Where do you come from? ¿De dónde es usted?

24

11
ˈkʌntrɪz ən ˈlæŋgwɪdʒɪz

ɪn ˈjʊərəp ðər ə ˈmenɪ ˈkʌntrɪz. ˈðəʊz wɪtʃ ə ˈnɪərɪst tə ˈspeɪn ə ˈpɔːtjʊgəl, ˈfrɑːns, ˈɪtəlɪ ən ˈgreɪt ˈbrɪtən. ðeɪ ˈspiːk ˌpɔːtjʊˈgiːz ɪn ˈpɔːtjʊgəl, ˈfrentʃ ɪn ˈfrɑːns, ɪˈtæljən ɪn ˈɪtəlɪ ən ˈɪŋglɪʃ ɪn ˈgreɪt ˈbrɪtən.

ɪn ˈspeɪn ðər ər ə ˈlɒt əv ˈtʊərɪsts ɪn ˈsʌmə. ðeɪ ˈkʌm frəm ˈdɪfrənt ˈkʌntrɪz, ɪsˈpeʃəlɪ frəm ˈfrɑːns, ˈdʒɜːmənɪ ən ˈgreɪt ˈbrɪtən. ðeɪ ˈkʌm tə ˈvɪzɪt ˈspeɪn.

ˈhɪər ɪz ə ˌkɒnvəˈseɪʃən bɪtwiːn ə ˈspæniəd ən səm ˈfɒrɪn ˈtʊərɪsts :-

****

- ˈwɒts jɔː ˈneɪm?
- maɪ ˈneɪmz ˈrɒbət.
- ˈweə dʊ jʊ ˈkʌm frɒm?
- aɪ ˈkʌm frəm ˈɪŋglənd. aɪm ˈɪŋglɪʃ. aɪ ˈspiːk ˈɪŋglɪʃ.

****

- ˈwɒts jɔː ˈneɪm?
- maɪ ˈneɪmz ˈʒak.
- ˈweə wə jʊ ˈbɔːn?
- aɪ wəz ˈbɔːn ɪn ˈfrɑːns. aɪm ˈfrentʃ. aɪ ˈspiːk ˈfrentʃ.

12
IN THE COUNTRY

In the country you can see mountains and valleys, rivers, fields, woods and meadows. In spring the trees are covered with buds and blossom. There is a lot of grass in the fields. In summer the trees are covered with leaves and fruit. In autumn the leaves fall. In winter the trees are bare.

Here is a conversation between a man from the town and a farmer:

- What are those trees in that orchard?
- They are fruit trees. This is an apple tree and that is a pear tree.
- What do strawberries grow on?
- They grow on small plants. Look, those are strawberries.
- What do you grow in this field?
- We grow wheat and barley here.
- What do you grow in the kitchen garden?
- We grow potatoes, cabbages, turnips and carrots.
- Do you grow any flowers?
- Oh, yes, we grow a lot of flowers in the garden, in front of the house.
- Are you happy in the country?
- Of course I'm very happy here! I have everything I want: milk, eggs, vegetables and fruit.
- I wish I lived in the country!

apple tree manzano
bare desnudo
barley cebada
blossom floración
buds capullos
cabbages coles
carrots zanahorias
eggs huevos

fall caerse
farmer granjero
fields campos
grass hierba
grow crecer, cultivar
kitchen garden huerta
leaves hojas
meadows prados

orchard huerto
pear tree peral
plants plantas
strawberries fresas
turnips nabos
valleys valles
wheat trigo
woods bosques

26

12

ɪn ðə ˈkʌntrɪ

ɪn ðə ˈkʌntrɪ jʊ kən ˈsiː ˈmaʊntənz ən ˈvælɪz, ˈrɪvəz, ˈfiːldz, ˈwʊdz ən ˈmedəʊz. ɪn ˈsprɪŋ ðə ˈtriːz ə ˈkʌvəd wɪð ˈbʌdz ən ˈblɒsəm. ðər ɪz ə ˈlɒt əv ˈgrɑːs ɪn ðə ˈfiːldz. ɪn ˈsʌmə ðə ˈtriːz ə ˈkʌvəd wɪð ˈliːvz ən ˈfruːt. ɪn ˈɔːtəm ðə ˈliːvz ˈfɔːl. ɪn ˈwɪntə ðə ˈtriːz ə ˈbeə.

ˈhɪər ɪz ə ˌkɒnvəˈseɪʃən bɪtwiːn ə ˈmæn frəm ðə ˈtaʊn ənd ə ˈfɑːmə :-

- ˈwɒt ə ðəʊz ˈtriːz ɪn ðæt ˈɔːtʃəd?
- ðeɪ ə ˈfruːt triːz. ˈðɪs ɪz ən ˈæpl triː ən ˈðæt ɪz ə ˈpeə triː
- ˈwɒt dʊ ˈstrɔːbərɪz ˈgrəʊ ɒn?
- ðeɪ ˈgrəʊ ɒn ˈsmɔːl ˈplɑːnts. ˈlʊk, ˈðəʊz ə ˈstrɔːbərɪz.
- ˈwɒt dʊ jʊ ˈgrəʊ ɪn ðɪs ˈfiːld?
- wɪ grəʊ ˈwiːt ən ˈbɑːlɪ hɪə.
- ˈwɒt dʊ jʊ ˈgrəʊ ɪn ðə ˌkɪtʃən ˈgɑːdən?
- wɪ grəʊ pəˈteɪtəʊz, ˈkæbɪdʒɪz, ˈtɜːnɪps ən ˈkærəts.
- dʊ jʊ ˈgrəʊ enɪ ˈflaʊəz?
- ˈəʊ, ˈjes, wɪ grəʊ ə ˈlɒt əv flaʊəz ɪn ðə ˈgɑːdən, ɪn ˈfrʌnt əv ðə ˈhaʊs.
- ə jʊ ˈhæpɪ ɪn ðə ˈkʌntrɪ?
- əv ˈkɔːs aɪm ˈverɪ ˈhæpɪ hɪə! aɪ hæv ˈevrɪθɪŋ aɪ ˈwɒnt :- ˈmɪlk, ˈegz, ˈvedʒətəblz ən ˈfruːt.
- aɪ ˈwɪʃ aɪ ˈlɪvd ɪn ðə ˈkʌntrɪ!

13
THE DAYS OF THE WEEK

There are seven days in a week.

The first day of the week is Monday. On Mondays we go back to work after the weekend. The second day of the week is Tuesday and the third is Wednesday. The fourth day is Thursday and the fifth is Friday. Saturday is the sixth day of the week. The seventh and last day of the week is Sunday.

On the subject of the days of the week, have you ever heard about the man who went to the doctor and said:

- Doctor, I have that Monday morning feeling.
- So do many people.
- Yes, doctor, but I have it every day.

****

THE DAYS OF THE WEEK

Monday, Tuesday, Wednesday, Thursday,
Friday, Saturday, Sunday.

every day cada día
feeling sensación
fifth quinto
first primero
fourth cuarto

go back volver
last último
morning matutino
second segundo
seven siete

sixth sexto
third tercero
week semana
weekend fin de semana
work trabajar

Have you ever heard about? ¿Han oído hablar alguna vez de?
So do many people Y mucha gente también.

28

13

ðə ˈdeɪz əv ðə ˈwiːk

ðər ə ˈsevən ˈdeɪz ɪn ə ˈwiːk.

ðə ˈfɜːst ˈdeɪ əv ðə ˈwiːk ɪz ˈmʌndɪ. ɒn ˈmʌndɪz wɪ ˈgəʊ
ˈbæk tə ˈwɜːk ɑːftə ðə ˌwiːkˈend. ðə ˈsekənd ˈdeɪ əv ðə ˈwiːk ɪz
ˈtjuːzdɪ ən ðə ˈθɜːd ɪz ˈwenzdɪ. ðə ˈfɔːθ ˈdeɪ ɪz ˈθɜːzdɪ ən
ðə ˈfɪfθ ɪz ˈfraɪdɪ. ˈsætədɪ ɪz ðə ˈsɪksθ ˈdeɪ əv ðə ˈwiːk.
ðə ˈsevənθ ən ˈlɑːst ˈdeɪ əv ðə ˈwiːk ɪz ˈsʌndɪ.

ɒn ðə ˈsʌbdʒɪkt əv ðə ˈdeɪz əv ðə ˈwiːk, həv ju ˈevə ˈhɜːd
əbaʊt ðə ˈmæn hʊ ˈwent tə ðə ˈdɒktə ən ˈsed :-

- ˈdɒktə, aɪ hæv ðæt ˈmʌndɪ mɔːnɪŋ ˈfiːlɪŋ.
- ˈsəʊ ˈduː menɪ ˈpiːpl.
- ˈjes, ˈdɒktə, bət aɪ hæv ɪt ˈevrɪ ˈdeɪ.

****

ðə ˈdeɪz əv ðə ˈwiːk

ˈmʌndɪ, ˈtjuːzdɪ, ˈwenzdɪ, ˈθɜːzdɪ,
ˈfraɪdɪ, ˈsætədɪ, ˈsʌndɪ

14
AT THE DENTIST'S

When you have toothache, you go to the dentist's. He has a look inside your mouth. If you have a very bad tooth, he will have to pull it out. If your tooth has a hole in it, he will fill it.

Here is a conversation between a patient and a dentist:

- Good morning.
- Good morning. Sit down here, please.
- I came because I've been having trouble with this tooth on the right.
- Let me have a look at it. Please open your mouth a little wider. Yes, I can see it now. It has a hole in it.
- Do you think you can save it?
- Yes, I think so. I shall have to fill it. Put your head a little to this side, will you?
- Will it hurt?
- No, the drill won't hurt at all.
- Ow! Ow!
- It will only take one more minute. There! It's all over. Rinse your mouth, please.
- I'm glad it's all over now!

drill taladro
fill empastar
hole agujero
hurt doler

mouth boca
patient paciente
pull out extraer
rinse enjuagarse

save salvar
tooth diente, muela
toothache dolor de muelas

It's all over now Ya todo ha acabado.
A little wider Un poco más.
Ow! Ow! ¡Ay! ¡Ay!

14
ət ðə 'dentɪsts

wen ju hæv 'tu:θeɪk, ju 'gəu tə ðə 'dentɪsts. hɪ hæz ə 'lʊk
ɪnsaɪd jɔ: 'mauθ. ɪf ju hæv ə 'verɪ bæd 'tu:θ, hɪ wɪl 'hæv tə
'pʊl ɪt 'aʊt. ɪf jɔ: 'tu:θ hæz ə 'həʊl ɪn ɪt, hɪ wɪl 'fɪl ɪt.

'hɪər ɪz ə ˌkɒnvə'seɪʃən bɪtwi:n ə 'peɪʃənt ənd ə 'dentɪst :-

- gʊd 'mɔ:nɪŋ.
- gʊd 'mɔ:nɪŋ. 'sɪt 'daʊn 'hɪə, 'pli:z.
- aɪ 'keɪm bɪkɒz aɪv bɪn 'hævɪŋ 'trʌbl wɪð ðɪs 'tu:θ
  ɒn ðə 'raɪt.
- 'let mɪ hæv ə 'lʊk ət ɪt. 'pli:z 'əʊpən jɔ: 'mauθ
  ə 'lɪtl 'waɪdə. 'jes, aɪ kən 'si: ɪt 'nau. ɪt hæz ə 'həʊl ɪn ɪt.
- du ju 'θɪŋk ju kən 'seɪv ɪt?
- 'jes, aɪ 'θɪŋk səʊ. aɪ ʃəl 'hæv tə 'fɪl ɪt. 'pʊt jɔ: 'hed
  ə 'lɪtl tə ðɪs 'saɪd, 'wɪl ju?
- wɪl ɪt 'hɜ:t?
- 'nəʊ, ðə 'drɪl wəʊnt 'hɜ:t ət 'ɔ:l.
- 'au! 'au!
- ɪt wɪl 'əʊnlɪ teɪk 'wʌn mɔ: 'mɪnɪt. 'ðeə! ɪts 'ɔ:l 'əʊvə.
  'rɪns jɔ: 'mauθ, 'pli:z.
- aɪm 'glæd ɪts 'ɔ:l 'əʊvə 'nau!

15
DIMENSIONS

- What are you going to do with that tape measure?
- I'm going to measure the length, the width and the height of this table.

- How long is the table? It's four feet, two inches long.
- How wide is the table? It's eighteen inches wide.
- How high is the table? It's two feet, seven inches high.

- What's the length of the table?
- The length of the table is four feet, two inches.
- What's the width of the table?
- The width of the table is eighteen inches.
- What's the height of the table?
- The height of the table is two feet, seven inches.

Look at the things around you and answer these questions:

- How long is this room?
- How wide is this table?
- How high is this chair?

feet pies	**length** longitud	**tape measure** metro
height altura	**long** largo	**wide** ancho
high alto	**measure** medir	**width** anchura

How long is...? ¿Cómo es de largo...?
How wide is...? ¿Cómo es de ancho...?
How high is...? ¿Cómo es de alto...?

What's the length of...? ¿Cuál es la longitud...?
What's the width of...? ¿Cuál es la anchura...?
What's the height of...? ¿Cuál es la altura...?

32

15
daɪˈmenʃənz

- 'wɒt ə ju 'gəʊɪŋ tə 'du: wɪð ðæt 'teɪp meʒə?
- aɪm gəʊɪŋ tə 'meʒə ðə 'leŋθ, ðə 'wɪdθ ən ðə 'haɪt əv ðɪs 'teɪbl.

- haʊ 'lɒŋ ɪz ðə 'teɪbl? ɪts 'fɔ: 'fi:t, 'tu: 'ɪntʃɪz lɒŋ.
- haʊ 'waɪd ɪz ðə 'teɪbl? ɪts 'eɪti:n 'ɪntʃɪz waɪd.
- haʊ 'haɪ ɪz ðə 'teɪbl? ɪts 'tu: 'fi:t, 'sevən 'ɪntʃɪz haɪ.

- 'wɒts ðə 'leŋθ əv ðə 'teɪbl?
- ðə 'leŋθ əv ðə 'teɪbl ɪz 'fɔ: 'fi:t, 'tu: 'ɪntʃɪz.
- 'wɒts ðə 'wɪdθ əv ðə 'teɪbl?
- ðə 'wɪdθ əv ðə 'teɪbl ɪz 'eɪti:n 'ɪntʃɪz.
- 'wɒts ðə 'haɪt əv ðə 'teɪbl?
- ðə 'haɪt əv ðə 'teɪbl ɪz 'tu: 'fi:t, 'sevən 'ɪntʃɪz.

'lʊk ət ðə 'θɪŋz ə'raʊnd ju ənd 'ɑ:nsə ði:z 'kwestʃənz :-

- haʊ 'lɒŋ ɪz ðɪs 'rʊm?
- haʊ 'waɪd ɪz ðɪs 'teɪbl?
- haʊ 'haɪ ɪz ðɪs 'tʃeə?

16
DINNER-TIME

It is a quarter to six. Mrs Wilson has already set the table for the family. There are four of them. She has put four plates on the table. Behind each plate, she has put a glass. On the right of each plate, she has put a knife and a spoon, and on the left side, a fork. In the middle of the table, there is a salt-cellar, a pot of pepper and a jug of water. There is also a bowl of salad, which she has prepared beforehand.

At six o'clock, the family come back home. They take off their coats, wash their hands, sit down at the table and begin dinner.

First the mother serves the soup. When they have finished, she takes away the plates and brings in the meat. It is a joint of lamb. She puts it on the table, carves it and gives a piece of meat to each person. Then she brings a dish of peas and a dish of roast potatoes and puts them in the middle of the table. Each of them takes a spoonful of peas or roast potatoes, according to what they like best.

After this course, Mrs Wilson tells her daughter Muriel to bring in the dessert. She goes to the kitchen and comes back with a bowl of fruit, which she puts on the table. The father takes a banana. The mother takes a pear. Susan takes an orange and Muriel takes an apple. As they eat, they talk about what they have done during the day.

carve trinchar	**knife** cuchillo	**salt-cellar** salero
course plato	**peas** guisantes	**serve** servir
dessert postre	**pepper** pimienta	**soup** sopa
fork tenedor	**piece** trozo	**spoon** cuchara
jug jarra	**roast** asado	**spoonful** cucharada
kitchen cocina	**salad** ensalada	**taste** probar

She takes away the plates Retira los platos.

34

16
'dɪnəˌtaɪm

ɪt ɪz ə 'kwɔ:tə tə 'sɪks. mɪsɪz 'wɪlsən həz ɔ:l'redɪ 'set ðə 'teɪbl fə ðə 'fæmɪlɪ. ðər ə 'fɔ: əv ðəm. ʃɪ həz 'pʊt 'fɔ: 'pleɪts ɒn ðə 'teɪbl. bɪhaɪnd 'i:tʃ 'pleɪt, ʃɪ həz 'pʊt ə 'glɑ:s. ɒn ðə 'raɪt əv i:tʃ 'pleɪt, ʃɪ həz 'pʊt ə 'naɪf ənd ə 'spu:n, ən ɒn ðə 'left 'saɪd, ə 'fɔ:k. ɪn ðə 'mɪdl əv ðə 'teɪbl, ðər ɪz ə 'sɔ:ltselə, ə 'pɒt əv 'pepə ənd ə 'dʒʌg əv 'wɔ:tə. ðər ɪz 'ɔ:lsəʊ ə 'bəʊl əv 'sæləd, wɪtʃ ʃɪ həz prɪ'peəd bɪ'fɔ:hænd.

ət 'sɪks əklɒk, ðə 'fæmɪlɪ 'kʌm bæk 'həʊm. ðeɪ 'teɪk ɒf ðeə 'kəʊts, 'wɒʃ ðeə 'hændz, 'sɪt 'daʊn ət ðə 'teɪbl ən bɪ'gɪn 'dɪnə.

'fɜ:st ðə 'mʌðə 'sɜ:vz ðə 'su:p. wen ðeɪ həv 'fɪnɪʃt, ʃɪ 'teɪks əweɪ ðə 'pleɪts ən 'brɪŋz 'ɪn ðə 'mi:t. ɪt ɪz ə 'dʒɔɪnt əv 'læm. ʃɪ 'pʊts ɪt ɒn ðə 'teɪbl, 'kɑ:vz ɪt ən 'gɪvz ə 'pi:s əv 'mi:t tʊ 'i:tʃ 'pɜ:sən. ðen ʃɪ 'brɪŋz ə 'dɪʃ əv 'pi:z ənd ə 'dɪʃ əv 'rəʊst pə'teɪtəʊz ən 'pʊts ðəm ɪn ðə 'mɪdl əv ðə 'teɪbl. 'i:tʃ əv ðəm 'teɪks ə 'spu:nfəl əv 'pi:z ɔ: 'rəʊst pə'teɪtəʊz, ə'kɔ:dɪŋ tə wɒt ðeɪ 'laɪk 'best.

ɑ:ftə ðɪs 'kɔ:s, mɪsɪz 'wɪlsən 'telz hə 'dɔ:tə 'mjʊrɪəl tə 'brɪŋ 'ɪn ðə dɪ'zɜ:t. ʃɪ 'gəʊz tə ðə 'kɪtʃən ən 'kʌmz 'bæk wɪð ə 'bəʊl əv 'fru:t, wɪtʃ ʃɪ 'pʊts ɒn ðə 'teɪbl. ðə 'fɑ:ðə 'teɪks ə bə'nɑ:nə. ðə 'mʌðə 'teɪks ə 'peə. 'su:zən 'teɪks ən 'ɒrɪndʒ ən 'mjʊrɪəl 'teɪks ən 'æpl. əz ðeɪ 'i:t, ðeɪ 'tɔ:k əbaʊt 'wɒt ðeɪ həv 'dʌn djʊərɪŋ ðə 'deɪ.

35

17
THE DOCTOR

Jim isn't feeling well today. He has a temperature. His mother tells him to go to bed and calls the doctor. The doctor comes and says:

- Tell me what the trouble is.
- I feel sick. I have a pain in my stomach and a headache.
- Let me take your temperature and your pulse. Give me your wrist, please.

Then the doctor examines Jim's stomach and asks him:

- Do you feel any pain here?
- A little.
- You mustn't eat anything today. Take this medicine three times a day. Tomorrow you can eat some vegetables and a little fish.
- How long must he take the medicine?
- For three days.
- Is it anything serious?
- Not at all. He will soon be well again. He will have to stay away from school for two days.

Jim is very happy when he hears the doctor's words. Then Jim's mother accompanies the doctor to the door to see him out.

- Goodbye.
- Goodbye, doctor.

call llamar	**pain** dolor	**sick** enfermo
headache dolor de cabeza	**pulse** pulso	**temperature** fiebre
	see out despedir	**wrist** muñeca

17
ðə ˈdɒktə

ˈdʒɪm ɪzənt ˈfiːlɪŋ ˈwel təˈdeɪ. hɪ hæz ə ˈtemprətʃə. hɪz
ˈmʌðə ˈtelz hɪm tə ˈɡəʊ tə ˈbed ən ˈkɔːlz ðə ˈdɒktə. ðə ˈdɒktə
ˈkʌmz ən ˈsez :-

- ˈtel mɪ ˈwɒt ðə ˈtrʌbl ɪz.
- aɪ ˈfiːl ˈsɪk. aɪ hæv ə ˈpeɪn ɪn maɪ ˈstʌmək ənd ə ˈhedeɪk.
- ˈlet mɪ ˈteɪk jɔː ˈtemprətʃə ən jɔː ˈpʌls. ˈɡɪv mɪ jɔː ˈrɪst,
  ˈpliːz.

ðen ðə ˈdɒktə ɪɡˈzæmɪnz ˈdʒɪmz ˈstʌmək ən ˈɑːsks hɪm :-

- dʊ jʊ ˈfiːl eni ˈpeɪn ˈhɪə?
- ə ˈlɪtl.
· - jʊ ˈmʌsnt iːt ˈeniθɪŋ təˈdeɪ. ˈteɪk ðɪs ˈmedsən ˈθriː ˈtaɪmz ə
  ˈdeɪ. təˈmɒrəʊ jʊ kən ˈiːt səm ˈvedʒətəblz ənd ə ˈlɪtl ˈfɪʃ.
- haʊ ˈlɒŋ məs hɪ ˈteɪk ðə ˈmedsən?
- fə ˈθriː ˈdeɪz.
- ɪz ɪt ˈeniθɪŋ ˈsɪərɪəs?
- ˈnɒt ət ˈɔːl. hɪ wɪl ˈsuːn bɪ ˈwel əˈɡeɪn. hɪ wɪl ˈhæv tə ˈsteɪ
  əˈweɪ frəm ˈskuːl fə ˈtuː ˈdeɪz.

ˈdʒɪm ɪz ˈverɪ ˈhæpɪ wen hɪ ˈhɪəz ðə ˈdɒktəz ˈwɜːdz. ðen
ˈdʒɪmz ˈmʌðə əˈkʌmpəniz ðə ˈdɒktə tə ðə ˈdɔː tə ˈsiː hɪm ˈaʊt.

- ɡʊdˈbaɪ.
- ɡʊdˈbaɪ, ˈdɒktə.

18

THE EARTH, THE SUN AND THE MOON

The earth is the planet where we live. The earth goes round the sun and the moon goes round the earth.

The sun rises in the east and sets in the west. When the sun rises, there is light. It is day. When the sun sets, there is no light. It is night.

The sun comes up in the morning and goes down in the afternoon or the evening, according to the country where it is seen and the season of the year. In Spain the sun goes down at about six p.m. in winter, when the days are short, or at about nine p.m. in summer, when the days are long.

The sun comes up in the east and travels towards the west. If you stand in the morning with the sun on your right-hand side, you face north and the south is behind you. At midday the sun is overhead. It is at its zenith, the highest point which it reaches in the sky. Then it begins to go down until it disappears in the west.

When the sun sets, the moon and the stars come out.

come out salir	**midday** mediodía	**set** ponerse
come up salir	**moon** luna	**sky** cielo
earth tierra	**night** noche	**south** sur
east este	**north** norte	**star** estrella
go down ponerse	**planet** planeta	**sun** sol
go round girar	**rise** levantarse	**west** oeste
light luz	**season** estación	**zenith** cenit

With the sun on your right-hand side Con el sol a su derecha.
The moon and the stars come out Salen la luna y las estrellas.

38

18
ðɪ ˈɜːθ, ðə ˈsʌn ən ðə ˈmuːn

ðɪ ˈɜːθ ɪz ðə ˈplænɪt weə wɪ ˈlɪv. ðɪ ˈɜːθ ˈgəʊz raʊnd ðə ˈsʌn ən ðə ˈmuːn gəʊz raʊnd ðɪ ˈɜːθ.

ðə ˈsʌn ˈraɪzɪz ɪn ðɪ ˈiːst ən ˈsets ɪn ðə ˈwest. wen ðə ˈsʌn ˈraɪzɪz, ðər ɪz ˈlaɪt. ɪt ɪz ˈdeɪ. wen ðə ˈsʌn ˈsets, ðər ɪz ˈnəʊ ˈlaɪt. ɪt ɪz ˈnaɪt.

ðə ˈsʌn kʌmz ˈʌp ɪn ðə ˈmɔːnɪŋ ən ˈgəʊz ˈdaʊn ɪn ðɪ ˌɑːftəˈnuːn ɔː ðɪ ˈiːvnɪŋ, əˈkɔːdɪŋ tə ðə ˈkʌntrɪ weər ɪt ɪz ˈsiːn ən ðə ˈsiːzən əv ðə ˈjɪə. ɪn ˈspeɪn ðə ˈsʌn gəʊz ˈdaʊn ət əbaʊt ˈsɪks ˈpiː ˈem ɪn ˈwɪntə, wen ðə ˈdeɪz ə ˈʃɔːt, ɔːr ət əbaʊt ˈnaɪn ˈpiː ˈem ɪn ˈsʌmə, wen ðə ˈdeɪz ə ˈlɒŋ.

ðə ˈsʌn kʌmz ˈʌp ɪn ðɪ ˈiːst ən ˈtrævəlz təwɔːdz ðə ˈwest. ɪf jʊ ˈstænd ɪn ðə ˈmɔːnɪŋ wɪð ðə ˈsʌn ɒn jɔː ˈraɪt hænd ˈsaɪd, jʊ ˈfeɪs ˈnɔːθ ən ðə ˈsaʊθ ɪz bɪˈhaɪnd jʊ. ət ˈmɪdeɪ ðə ˈsʌn ɪz ˌəʊvəˈhed. ɪt ɪz ət ɪts ˈzenɪθ, ðə ˈhaɪɪst ˈpɔɪnt wɪtʃ ɪt ˈriːtʃɪz ɪn ðə ˈskaɪ. ðen ɪt bɪˈgɪnz tə gəʊ ˈdaʊn ʌntɪl ɪt ˌdɪsəˈpɪəz ɪn ðə ˈwest.

wen ðə ˈsʌn ˈsets, ðə ˈmuːn ən ðə ˈstɑːz kʌm ˈaʊt.

19
EVERYDAY ACTIONS

Everybody does the same things every day. Let's take Mr Slater, for example: He gets up at eight o'clock in the morning. He washes and shaves. Then he dresses. After that he has breakfast.

After breakfast he leaves home and goes to the office. He usually takes the bus. He gets to his office at nine o'clock. He works until one, when he goes to a snack bar near his office to have something to eat. He generally eats the same thing: a cheese sandwich or a hamburger with a glass of beer. Then he goes back to work until five, when the bell rings for the people to stop work. At that moment he tidies up his desk, puts on his coat and walks out of the office.

He goes to the bus stop, which is just around the corner, and catches the bus home. On the bus he reads the paper. When he arrives home, his wife and children are waiting for him. He takes off his coat. He also takes off his shoes and puts on a pair of slippers. Then he sits down in an armchair.

His children come and ask him questions about their homework. A moment later, his wife calls him and the children for dinner. After dinner, he and his wife sit down to watch television for about an hour. Then the family go to bed.

breakfast desayuno	**office** oficina	**tidy up** asear
catch tomar (autobús)	**paper** periódico	**walk out** salir
corner esquina	**read** leer	**wash** lavarse
dress vestirse	**shave** afeitarse	**watch television** ver la
get up levantarse	**sit down** sentarse	televisión
leave salir	**slippers** zapatillas	**work** trabajo, trabajar

19
'evrɪdeɪ 'ækʃənz

'evrɪˌbɒdɪ 'dʌz ðə 'seɪm 'θɪŋz 'evrɪ 'deɪ. 'lets 'teɪk mɪstə 'sleɪtə,
fər ɪgˈzɑːmpl :- hɪ 'gets 'ʌp ət 'eɪt əklɒk ɪn ðə 'mɔːnɪŋ. hɪ
'wɒʃɪz ən 'ʃeɪvz. ðen hɪ 'dresɪz. ɑːftə 'ðæt hɪ hæz 'brekfəst.

ɑːftə 'brekfəst hɪ 'liːvz 'həum ən 'gəuz tə ðɪ 'ɒfɪs. hɪ
'juːʒuəlɪ 'teɪks ðə 'bʌs. hɪ 'gets tə ðɪ 'ɒfɪs ət 'naɪn əklɒk. hɪ
'wɜːks ʌntɪl 'wʌn, wen hɪ 'gəuz tu ə 'snæk bɑː: nɪə hɪz 'ɒfɪs
tə hæv 'sʌmθɪŋ tu 'iːt. hɪ 'dʒenərəlɪ 'iːts ðə 'seɪm 'θɪŋ :-
ə 'tʃiːz 'sænwɪdʒ ɔːr ə 'hæmˌbɜːgə wɪð ə 'glɑːs əv 'bɪə. ðen
hɪ 'gəuz 'bæk tə 'wɜːk ʌntɪl 'faɪv, wen ðə 'bel 'rɪŋz
fə ðə 'piːpl tə 'stɒp 'wɜːk. ət ðæt 'məumənt hɪ 'taɪdɪz ʌp hɪz
'desk, 'puts ɒn hɪz 'kəut ən 'wɔːks aut əv ðɪ 'ɒfɪs.

hɪ 'gəuz tə ðə 'bʌs stɒp, wɪtʃ ɪz 'dʒʌst əraund ðə 'kɔːnə,
ən 'kætʃɪz ðə 'bʌs 'həum. ɒn ðə 'bʌs hɪ 'riːdz ðə 'peɪpə.
wen hɪ ə'raɪvz 'həum, hɪz 'waɪf ən 'tʃɪldrən ə 'weɪtɪŋ fə
hɪm. hɪ 'teɪks ɒf hɪz 'kəut. hɪ 'ɔːlsəu 'teɪks ɒf hɪz 'ʃuːz
ən 'puts ɒn ə 'peər əv 'slɪpəz. ðen hɪ 'sɪts 'daun ɪn ən
ˌɑːmˈtʃeə.

hɪz 'tʃɪldrən 'kʌm ən 'ɑːsk hɪm 'kwestʃənz əbaut ðeə
'həumwɜːk. ə 'məumənt 'leɪtə, hɪz 'waɪf 'kɔːlz hɪm ən ðə
'tʃɪldrən fə 'dɪnə. ɑːftə 'dɪnə, 'hiː ən hɪz 'waɪf sɪt 'daun
tə 'wɒtʃ 'telɪˌvɪʒən fər əbaut ən 'auə. ðen ðə 'fæmɪlɪ
'gəu tə 'bed.

20
THE FIVE SENSES

We have five senses: sight, hearing, smell, taste and touch.

The eyes are the organs of sight. The ears are the organs of hearing. The nose is the organ of smell. The tongue and the palate are the organs of taste, and the skin contains the organs of touch.

We see with our eyes. We hear with our ears. We smell with our nose. We taste with our tongue and palate. We touch with our fingers.

In order to live, we must eat, drink and breathe. We eat when we are hungry, and we drink when we are thirsty.

We breathe continuously. We never stop breathing. A person stops breathing when he dies.

We see people, things and animals.
We hear music, noises and sounds.
We smell flowers and perfume.
We taste food and drink.
We touch people, things and animals.

breathe respirar
die morir
drink beber
ear oreja
eat comer
eye ojo
finger dedo
hear oír

hearing oído
hungry hambriento
noise ruido
nose nariz
organs órganos
palate paladar
see ver
sense sentido

sight vista
skin piel
smell olfato, oler
sound sonido
taste gusto, catar
thirsty sediento
tongue lengua
touch tacto, tocar

When we are hungry Cuando tenemos hambre.
When we are thirsty Cuando tenemos sed.

20
ðə 'faɪv 'sensɪz

wɪ hæv 'faɪv 'sensɪz :- 'saɪt, 'hɪərɪŋ, 'smel, 'teɪst ən 'tʌtʃ.

ðɪ 'aɪz ə ðɪ 'ɔ:gənz əv 'saɪt. ðɪ 'ɪəz ə ðɪ 'ɔ:gənz əv 'hɪərɪŋ.
ðə 'nəʊz ɪz ðɪ 'ɔ:gən əv 'smel. ðə 'tʌŋ ən ðə 'pælɪt ə ðɪ
'ɔ:gənz əv 'teɪst, ən ðə 'skɪn kən'teɪnz ðɪ 'ɔ:gənz əv 'tʌtʃ.

wɪ 'si: wɪð aʊər 'aɪz. wɪ 'hɪə wɪð aʊər 'ɪəz. wɪ 'smel wɪð
aʊə 'nəʊz. wɪ 'teɪst wɪð aʊə 'tʌŋ ən 'pælɪt. wɪ 'tʌtʃ wɪð aʊə
'fɪŋgəz.

ɪn 'ɔ:də tə 'lɪv, wɪ məst 'i:t, 'drɪŋk ən 'bri:ð. wɪ 'i:t wen
wɪ ə 'hʌŋgrɪ, ən wɪ 'drɪŋk wen wɪ ə 'θɜ:stɪ.

wɪ 'bri:ð kən'tɪnjʊəslɪ. wɪ 'nevə 'stɒp 'bri:ðɪŋ. ə 'pɜ:sən
'stɒps 'bri:ðɪŋ wen hɪ 'daɪz.

wɪ 'si: 'pi:pl, 'θɪŋz ənd 'ænɪməlz.
wɪ 'hɪə 'mju:zɪk, 'nɔɪzɪz ən 'saʊndz.
wɪ 'smel 'flaʊəz ən 'pɜ:fju:m.
wɪ 'teɪst 'fu:d ən 'drɪŋk.
wɪ 'tʌtʃ 'pi:pl, 'θɪŋz ənd 'ænɪməlz.

21
FOOD AND DRINKS

We would die without food and drink. Food is what can be eaten by people or animals. We drink water, milk, tea and coffee.

We must choose carefully the food we eat. Meat, fish and eggs provide us with protein, which is necessary for good health. Vegetables and fruit are valuable for their mineral salts and vitamins.

There are green vegetables, such as peas, French beans, cabbage, cauliflower and spinach, and root vegetables, such as carrots, turnips and potatoes. A salad made of tomato, lettuce, onion and cucumber is rich in vitamins and very good for your health.

On the subject of fruit, we must mention oranges, lemons, strawberries, grapes, melon, water melon, apples, pears and bananas.

Food can be eaten raw or cooked. The art or practice of cooking is called cookery. There are lots of cookery books which give you information about how to cook food.

We should not drink alcoholic drinks, such as brandy, gin, rum and whisky. They are very bad for the health. Some people drink a little wine or beer with their meals, which is not a bad thing if you drink just a little.

cauliflower coliflor	**grapes** uvas	**raw** crudo
cooked cocinado	**health** salud	**root vegetables**
cookery cocina (arte)	**lettuce** lechuga	tubérculos
cucumber pepino	**meal** comida	**rum** ron
food alimento	**melon** melón	**spinach** espinacas
French beans judías	**onion** cebolla	**valuable** valioso
verdes	**protein** proteínas	**water melon** sandía

21
'fu:d ən 'drɪŋks

wɪ wəd 'daɪ wɪðaut 'fu:d ən 'drɪŋk. 'fu:d ɪz wɒt kən bɪ 'i:tən baɪ 'pi:pl ɔ:r 'ænɪməlz. wɪ 'drɪŋk 'wɔ:tə, 'mɪlk, 'ti: ən 'kɒfɪ.

wɪ məs 'tʃu:z 'keəfəlɪ ðə 'fu:d wɪ 'i:t. 'mi:t, 'fɪʃ ənd 'egz prə'vaɪd əs wɪð 'prəuti:n, wɪtʃ ɪz 'nesəsərɪ fə 'gud 'helθ. 'vedʒətəblz ən 'fru:t ə 'væljuəbl fə ðeə 'mɪnərəl 'sɔ:lts ən 'vɪtəmɪnz.

ðər ə 'gri:n 'vedʒətəblz, sʌtʃ əz 'pi:z, ˌfrentʃ 'bi:nz, 'kæbɪdʒ, 'kɒlɪˌflauə ən 'spɪnɪdʒ, ən 'ru:t 'vedʒətəblz, sʌtʃ əz 'kærəts, 'tɜ:nɪps ən pə'teɪtəuz. ə 'sæləd 'meɪd əv tə'ma:təu, 'letɪs, 'ʌnjən ən 'kju:kʌmbə ɪz 'rɪtʃ ɪn 'vɪtəmɪnz ən 'verɪ 'gud fə jɔ: 'helθ.

ɒn ðə 'sʌbdʒɪkt əv 'fru:t, wɪ məs 'menʃən 'ɒrɪndʒɪz, 'lemənz, 'strɔ:bərɪz, 'greɪps, 'melən, 'wɔ:tə ˌmelən, 'æplz, 'peəz ən bə'na:nəz.

'fu:d kən bɪ 'i:tən 'rɔ: ɔ: 'kukt. ðɪ 'a:t ɔ: 'præktɪs əv 'kukɪŋ ɪz 'kɔ:ld 'kukərɪ. ðər ə 'lɒts əv 'kukərɪ ˌbuks wɪtʃ 'gɪv ju ˌɪnfə'meɪʃən əbaut 'hau tə 'kuk 'fu:d.

wɪ ʃəd 'nɒt 'drɪŋk ˌælkə'hɒlɪk 'drɪŋks, sʌtʃ əz 'brændɪ, 'dʒɪn, 'rʌm ən 'wɪskɪ. ðeɪ ə 'verɪ 'bæd fə ðə 'helθ. 'sʌm 'pi:pl 'drɪŋk ə 'lɪtl 'waɪn ɔ: 'bɪə wɪð ðeə 'mi:lz, wɪtʃ ɪz 'nɒt ə 'bæd 'θɪŋ ɪf ju 'drɪŋk dʒʌst ə 'lɪtl.

22
AT THE HAIRDRESSER'S

When your hair is too long, you go to the hairdresser's.

Sometimes there are some people waiting to be attended to, and you have to wait a few minutes. Meanwhile you can read newspapers or magazines which are usually lying on a table. A customer comes into a hairdresser's:

- Good morning.
- Good morning, sir.
- How long will I have to wait?
- You won't have to wait long, sir. About ten minutes.
- O.K. I'll wait then.

The customer sits down, picks up a newspaper and begins to read it. A few minutes later, the hairdresser says to him:

- I'm ready, sir. Haircut?
- Yes, please.
- Would you like your hair cut short?
- Yes, short back and sides.

Twenty minutes later, the hairdresser hands a mirror to the customer and says:

- How d'you like it, sir?
- It's fine. That's just the way I like it.

Then the customer pays the hairdresser, puts on his coat and goes out.

customer parroquiano	**haircut** corte de pelo	**hand** entregar
cut cortar, cortado	**hairdresser** peluquero	**mirror** espejo

22
ət ðə ˈheəˌdresəz

wen jɔ: ˈheər ɪz ˈtu: ˈlɒŋ, ju ˈgəu tə ðə ˈheəˌdresəz.

ˈsʌmtaɪmz ðər ə səm ˈpi:pl ˈweɪtɪŋ tə bɪ əˈtendɪd tu, ənd ju ˈhæv tə weɪt ə ˈfju: ˈmɪnɪts. ˈmi:nwaɪl ju kən ˈri:d ˈnju:sˌpeɪpəz ɔ: ˌmægəˈzi:nz wɪtʃ ə ˈju:ʒuəlɪ ˈlaɪɪŋ ɒn ə ˈteɪbl. ə ˈkʌstəmə ˈkʌmz ɪntu ə ˈheəˌdresəz :-
- gud ˈmɔ:nɪŋ.
- gud ˈmɔ:nɪŋ, sə.
- hau ˈlɒŋ wɪl aɪ ˈhæv tə ˈweɪt?
- ju ˈwəunt hæv tə ˈweɪt ˈlɒŋ, sə. əbaut ˈten ˈmɪnɪts.
- ˈəu ˈkeɪ. aɪl ˈweɪt ðen.

ðə ˈkʌstəmə sɪts ˈdaun, ˈpɪks ʌp ə ˈnju:sˌpeɪpə ən bɪˈgɪnz tə ˈri:d ɪt. ə ˈfju: mɪnɪts ˈleɪtə, ðə ˈheəˌdresə ˈsez tə hɪm :-
- aɪm ˈredɪ, sə. ˈheəkʌt?
- ˈjes, ˈpli:z.
- wud ju ˈlaɪk jɔ: ˈheə ˈkʌt ˈʃɔ:t?
- ˈjes, ˈʃɔ:t ˈbæk ən ˈsaɪdz.

ˈtwentɪ mɪnɪts ˈleɪtə, ðə ˈheəˌdresə ˈhændz ə ˈmɪrə tə ðə ˈkʌstəmə ən ˈsez :-
- ˈhau dju ˈlaɪk ɪt, sə?
- ɪts ˈfaɪn. ˈðæts ˈdʒʌst ðə ˈweɪ aɪ ˈlaɪk ɪt.

ðen ðə ˈkʌstəmə ˈpeɪz ðə ˈheəˌdresə, ˈputs ɒn hɪz ˈkəut ən ˈgəuz ˈaut.

23
HOBBIES

Most English people have an indoor hobby of some kind. The reason may be that winter evenings in England are very long and people cannot go outside to enjoy nature.

Hobbies are quite widespread in England and they are becoming common in Spain, too.

People like collecting things, such as stamps, coins, postcards and razor blade wrappers. There are other hobbies, too, such as painting or playing a musical instrument.

My friend James is a stamp-collector. He has about two thousand stamps from many countries. He enjoys looking at his stamps through a magnifying glass.

My friend David is an amateur photographer. He has a good camera and enjoys taking photographs and developing them in his own darkroom.

Having a hobby is very interesting. It keeps you busy and prevents you from getting bored.

bored aburrido	**magnifying glass** lupa	**reason** motivo
busy ocupado	**most** la mayoría	**spread** extendido
darkroom cuarto oscuro	**prevent** evitar	**stamps** sellos
	razor blade hoja de afeitar	**widespread** extendido
enjoy disfrutar		**wrapper** envoltorio

And enjoys taking photograhs Y disfruta haciendo fotos.
It keeps you busy Te mantiene ocupado.

23
'hɒbɪz

'məʊst 'ɪŋglɪʃ 'pi:pl hæv ən 'ɪndɔ: 'hɒbɪ əv 'sʌm 'kaɪnd. ðə 'ri:zən meɪ 'bi: ðət 'wɪntə 'i:vnɪŋz ɪn 'ɪŋglənd ə 'verɪ 'lɒŋ ən 'pi:pl 'kænɒt gəʊ aʊt'saɪd tʊ ɪn'dʒɔɪ 'neɪtʃə.

'hɒbɪz ə 'kwaɪt 'waɪspred ɪn 'ɪŋglənd ən ðeɪ ə bɪ'kʌmɪŋ 'kɒmən ɪn 'speɪn, 'tu:

'pi:pl 'laɪk kə'lektɪŋ 'θɪŋz, sʌtʃ əz 'stæmps, 'kɔɪnz, 'pəʊstkɑ:dz ən 'reɪzə bleɪd 'ræpəz. ðər ə 'ʌðə 'hɒbɪz, 'tu:, sʌtʃ əz 'peɪntɪŋ ɔ: 'pleɪɪŋ ə 'mju:zɪkl 'ɪnstrəmənt.

maɪ 'frend 'dʒeɪmz ɪz ə 'stæmp kə,lektə. hɪ hæz əbaʊt 'tu: θaʊzənd 'stæmps frəm 'menɪ 'kʌntrɪz. hɪ ɪn'dʒɔɪz 'lʊkɪŋ ət hɪz 'stæmps θru: ə 'mægnɪfaɪɪŋ ,glɑ:s.

maɪ 'frend 'deɪvɪd ɪz ən 'æmətə fə'tɒgrəfə. hɪ hæz ə 'gʊd 'kæmərə ən ɪn'dʒɔɪz 'teɪkɪŋ 'fəʊtəgrɑ:fs ən dɪ'veləpɪŋ ðəm ɪn hɪz 'əʊn 'dɑ:krʊm.

'hævɪŋ ə 'hɒbɪ ɪz 'verɪ 'ɪntrɪstɪŋ. ɪt 'ki:ps jʊ 'bɪzɪ ən prɪ'vents jʊ frəm 'getɪŋ 'bɔ:d.

24
HOLIDAYS

- Where are you going for your holidays this year?

- We'll probably be going to the seaside.

- You go to the seaside every year. Why don't you go to the country for a change?

- Well, my wife likes the sea, and the children like to play on the beach.

- But, which do you prefer, the sea or the country?

- I prefer the country to the sea. I don't like the sea. I can't swim. All I want to do is rest and be away from the smoke of the town. Besides, the sea is a long way from here, and the country is only a few miles away. In fact, I don't know where we shall go this year. What about you? Where are you going?

- We've bought a tent and we intend to spend the summer at a camping site.

beach playa	**country** campo	**seaside** costa
bought comprado	**holidays** vacaciones	**swim** nadar
camping site 'camping'	**sea** mar	**tent** tienda de campaña

What about you? ¿Y tú?
For a change Para variar.
In fact De hecho
We intend to spend the summer Tenemos la intención de pasar el verano.

24
'hɒlɪdeɪz

- 'weər ə jʊ 'gəʊɪŋ fə jɔː 'hɒlɪdeɪz ðɪs 'jɪə?

- wiːl 'prɒbəblɪ bɪ 'gəʊɪŋ tə ðə 'siːsaɪd.

- jʊ 'gəʊ tə ðə 'siːsaɪd 'evrɪ 'jɪə. 'waɪ dəʊnt jʊ 'gəʊ tə ðə 'kʌntrɪ fər ə 'tʃeɪndʒ?

- 'wel, maɪ 'waɪf laɪks ðə 'siː, ən ðə 'tʃɪldrən laɪk tə 'pleɪ ɒn ðə 'biːtʃ.

- bət, 'wɪtʃ dʊ jʊ prɪ'fɜː, ðə 'siː ɔː ðə 'kʌntrɪ?

- aɪ prɪ'fɜː ðə 'kʌntrɪ tə ðə 'siː - aɪ 'dəʊnt laɪk ðə 'siː - aɪ 'kɑːnt 'swɪm. 'ɔːl aɪ 'wɒnt tə 'duː ɪz 'rest ən bɪ ə'weɪ frəm ðə 'sməʊk əv ðə 'taʊn. bɪ'saɪdz, ðə 'siː ɪz ə 'lɒŋ 'weɪ frəm 'hɪə, ən ðə 'kʌntrɪ ɪz 'əʊnlɪ ə 'fjuː 'maɪlz ə'weɪ. ɪn 'fækt, aɪ 'dəʊn nəʊ 'weə wɪ ʃəl 'gəʊ ðɪs 'jɪə. 'wɒt əbaʊt 'juː? 'weər ə jʊ 'gəʊɪŋ?

- wiːv 'bɔːt ə 'tent ən wɪ ɪn'tend tə spend ðə 'sʌmə ət ə 'kæmpɪŋ ˌsaɪt.

25
AT THE HOSPITAL

When we have to be operated on, we are taken to a hospital. In the town where I live there is a very big hospital.

A fortnight ago, I went there to visit Tim, a schoolmate who had been operated on for appendicitis.

As I walked down the long corridors of the hospital, I saw a lot of doctors and nurses coming and going. There were several wards with sick people in them. On one door there were the words "Operating Theatre."

Tim told me that the surgeon was very good and that he had not felt anything at all. He also said that as soon as he was lying on the operating table, a nurse gave him an injection and put him to sleep. When he woke up, it was all over.

He recovered from the operation in a few days, and now he is walking again.

ago hace   **lying** tumbado   **ward** sala de hospital
corridors pasillos   **put** poner, puesto   **woke up** se despertó
fortnight quincena   **surgeon** cirujano   **words** palabras

It was all over Todo había acabado.

25
ət ðə ˈhɒspɪtəl

wen wɪ ˈhæv tə bɪ ˈɒpəreɪtɪd ˈɒn, wɪ ə ˈteɪkən tʊ ə ˈhɒspɪtəl. ɪn ðə ˈtaʊn weər aɪ ˈlɪv ðər ɪz ə ˈverɪ bɪg ˈhɒspɪtəl.

ə ˈfɔːtnaɪt əˈgəʊ, aɪ ˈwent ˈðeə tə ˈvɪzɪt ˈtɪm, ə ˈskuːlmeɪt hʊ həd bɪn ˈɒpəreɪtɪd ˈɒn fər əˌpendɪˈsaɪtɪs.

æz aɪ ˈwɔːkt daʊn ðə ˈlɒŋ ˈkɒrɪdɔːz əv ðə ˈhɒspɪtəl, aɪ ˈsɔː ə ˈlɒt əv ˈdɒktəz ən ˈnɜːsɪz ˈkʌmɪŋ ən ˈgəʊɪŋ. ðə wə ˈsevərəl ˈwɔːdz wɪð ˈsɪk ˈpiːpl ɪn ðəm. ɒn ˈwʌn ˈdɔː ðə wə ðə ˈwɜːdz :- ˈɒpəreɪtɪŋ ˌθɪətə.

ˈtɪm ˈtəʊld mɪ ðət ðə ˈsɜːdʒən wəz ˈverɪ ˈgʊd ən ðət hɪ həd ˈnɒt ˈfelt ˈenɪθɪŋ ət ˈɔːl. hɪ ˈɔːlsəʊ ˈsed ðət əz ˈsuːn əz hɪ wəz ˈlaɪɪŋ ɒn ðɪ ˈɒpəreɪtɪŋ ˌteɪbl, ə ˈnɜːs ˈgeɪv hɪm ən ɪnˈdʒekʃən ən ˈpʊt hɪm tə ˈsliːp. wen hɪ ˈwəʊk ˈʌp, ɪt wəz ˈɔːl ˈəʊvə.

hɪ rɪˈkʌvəd frəm ðɪ ˌɒpəˈreɪʃən ɪn ə ˈfjuː ˈdeɪz, ən ˈnaʊ hɪ ɪz ˈwɔːkɪŋ əˈgeɪn.

26
AT THE HOTEL

A hotel is a building where meals and rooms are provided for travellers. When you go into a hotel, you see the reception desk with the receptionist behind it.

Here is a conversation between a traveller and a receptionist:

- Good evening. Do you have a room?
- Yes, sir. Double or single?
- A single, please.
- I have a single room on the first floor.
- Is it at the front or back?
- It's at the front.
- Couldn't you give me one at the back? This street is very noisy.
- Yes, sir. There's another room at the back, but it's on the seventh floor.
- That will be all right. How much is it for bed and breakfast?
- Thirty pounds.
- Okay.
- Room number 75. Will you sign here, please?

The guest signs the register. The receptionist calls the bellboy, hands him a key and tells him to accompany the guest to his room. Then the bellboy takes the traveller's luggage and says to him:
- This way, sir.

The bellboy shows the guest into his room, puts the luggage on the rack, and the guest gives him a tip. Then the bellboy says:
- Thank you, sir.

bellboy botones   **guest** huésped   **noisy** ruidosa
double doble   **luggage** equipaje   **register** registro

26
ət ðə həʊˈtel

ə həʊˈtel ɪz ə ˈbɪldɪŋ weə ˈmi:lz ən ˈrʊmz ə prəˈvaɪdɪd fə ˈtrævələz. wen jʊ ˈɡəʊ ɪntʊ ə həʊˈtel, jʊ ˈsi: ðə rɪˈsepʃən ˌdesk wɪð ðə rɪˈsepʃənɪst bɪˈhaɪnd ɪt.

ˈhɪər ɪz ə ˌkɒnvəˈseɪʃən bɪtwi:n ə ˈtrævələ ənd ə rɪˈsepʃənɪst :-

- gʊd ˈi:vnɪŋ. dʊ jʊ hæv ə ˈrʊm?
- ˈjes, sə. ˈdʌbl ɔ: ˈsɪŋgl?
- ə ˈsɪŋgl, ˈpli:z.
- aɪ hæv ə ˈsɪŋgl ˈrʊm ɒn ðə ˈfɜ:st ˈflɔ:
- ɪz ɪt ət ðə ˈfrʌnt ɔ: ˈbæk?
- ɪts ət ðə ˈfrʌnt.
- ˈkʊdənt jʊ ˈgɪv mɪ ˈwʌn ət ðə ˈbæk? ðɪs ˈstri:t ɪz ˈverɪ ˈnɔɪzɪ.
- ˈjes, sə. ðəz əˈnʌðə ˈrʊm ət ðə ˈbæk, bət ɪts ɒn ðə ˈsevənθ ˈflɔ:
- ˈðæt wɪl bɪ ɔ:l ˈraɪt. ˈhaʊ ˈmʌtʃ ɪz ɪt fə ˈbed ən ˈbrekfəst?
- ˈθɜ:tɪ ˈpaʊndz.
- ˈəʊˈkeɪ.
- ˈrʊm ˈnʌmbə sevəntɪ ˈfaɪv. wɪl jʊ ˈsaɪn ˈhɪə, ˈpli:z?

ðə ˈgest ˈsaɪnz ðə ˈredʒɪstə. ðə rɪˈsepʃənɪst ˈkɔ:lz ðə ˈbelbɔɪ, ˈhændz hɪm ə ˈki: ən ˈtelz hɪm tʊ əˈkʌmpənɪ ðə ˈgest tə hɪz ˈrʊm. ðen ðə ˈbelbɔɪ ˈteɪks ðə ˈtrævələz ˈlʌgɪdʒ ən ˈsez tə hɪm :-
- ðɪs ˈweɪ, sə.

ðə ˈbelbɔɪ ˈʃəʊz ðə ˈgest ɪntə hɪz ˈrʊm, ˈpʊts ðə ˈlʌgɪdʒ ɒn ðə ˈræk, ən ðə ˈgest ˈgɪvz hɪm ə ˈtɪp. ðen ðə ˈbelbɔɪ ˈsez :-
- ˈθæŋk jʊ, sə.

27
THE HUMAN BODY

Jim asks his father:

- Can you show me how to draw a man, daddy?

- Yes, let me see... First, you draw the head. The head is on the shoulders. The hair is on the head. The nose is between the eyes and the mouth. The nose is above the mouth, so the mouth is below the nose. The chin is below the mouth. Then, the ears: The right ear and the left ear. The neck is between the head and the shoulders. Now, let's draw the body. The chest is in front and the back is behind.

- What about the arms and the legs?

- First, we'll draw the arms, the hands and the fingers. We have ten fingers altogether on both hands. Then, the legs, the knees and the feet. We have five toes on each foot.

above encima de	**ears** orejas	**knees** rodillas
arms brazos	**eye** ojo	**legs** piernas
back espalda	**feet** pies	**mouth** boca
below debajo de	**fingers** dedos	**neck** cuello
behind detrás	**hair** pelo	**nose** nariz
chest pecho	**hands** manos	**shoulders** hombros
chin barbilla	**head** cabeza	**toes** dedos del pie

What about the arms and the legs? ¿Y los brazos y las piernas?

27
ðə ˈhjuːmən ˈbɒdɪ

ˈdʒɪm ˈɑːsks hɪz ˈfɑːðə :-

- kən juː ˈʃəu mɪ ˈhau tə ˈdrɔː ə ˈmæn, ˈdædɪ?

- ˈjes, ˈlet mɪ ˈsiː ... ˈfɜːst, juː ˈdrɔː ðə ˈhed. ðə ˈhed ɪz ɒn ðə ˈʃəuldəz. ðə ˈheər ɪz ɒn ðə ˈhed. ðə ˈnəuz ɪz bɪtwiːn ðɪ ˈaɪz ən ðə ˈmauθ. ðə ˈnəuz ɪz əbʌv ðə ˈmauθ, səu ðə ˈmauθ ɪz bɪləu ðə ˈnəuz. ðə ˈtʃɪn ɪz bɪləu ðə ˈmauθ. ðen, ðɪ ˈɪəz :- ðə ˈraɪt ˈɪə ən ðə ˈleft ɪə. ðə ˈnek ɪz bɪtwiːn ðə ˈhed ən ðə ˈʃəuldəz. nau, ˈlets ˈdrɔː ðə ˈbɒdɪ. ðə ˈtʃest ɪz ɪn ˈfrʌnt ən ðə ˈbæk ɪz bɪˈhaɪnd.

- ˈwɒt əbaut ðɪ ˈɑːmz ən ðə ˈlegz?

- ˈfɜːst, wiːl ˈdrɔː ðɪ ˈɑːmz, ðə ˈhændz ən ðə ˈfɪŋgəz. wɪ hæv ˈten ˈfɪŋgəz ˌɔːltəˈgeðə ɒn ˈbəuθ ˈhændz. ðen, ðə ˈlegz, ðə ˈniːz ən ðə ˈfiːt. wɪ hæv ˈfaɪv ˈtəuz ɒn ˈiːtʃ ˈfut.

28
MEALS

Every day we have four meals. English people divide the meals as follows:

The first meal of the day is breakfast, which they have between eight and nine. It usually consists of bacon and eggs together with buttered toast and marmalade. They drink either tea or coffee at breakfast.

The second meal of the day is lunch, which they have between twelve and one. People who work in offices and factories often have lunch in a snack bar near their work. It generally consists of a salad made of tomatoes, lettuce and cucumber with some cold meat, or perhaps a cheese sandwich and some beer.

In the afternoon, between four and five, they have tea with cakes or thin slices of bread and butter with jam.

The last meal of the day is supper, which is served at about half-past six. Then all the members of the family sit together. At supper they eat soup, fish or meat with vegetables, such as peas or French beans. For dessert they eat various kinds of fruit, such as bananas, oranges, pears or a pudding.

bread pan
breakfast desayuno
butter mantequilla
cake pastel, tarta
jam confitura

marmalade mermelada de naranja
perhaps tal vez
salad ensalada
slices rebanadas

soup sopa
supper cena
thin fino, delgado
toast tostada
together juntos

As follows Como sigue.
Either .... or... O ... o ..

28
'mi:lz

'evrɪ 'deɪ wɪ hæv 'fɔ: 'mi:lz. 'ɪŋglɪʃ 'pi:pl dɪ'vaɪd ðə 'mi:lz əz 'fɒləʊz :-

ðə 'fɜ:st 'mi:l əv ðə 'deɪ ɪz 'brekfəst, wɪtʃ ðeɪ hæv bɪtwi:n 'eɪt ən 'naɪn. ɪt 'ju:ʒʊəlɪ kən'sɪsts əv 'beɪkən ənd 'egz tə'geðə wɪð 'bʌtəd 'təʊst ən 'ma:məleɪd. ðeɪ 'drɪŋk aɪðə 'ti: ɔ: 'kɒfɪ ət 'brekfəst.

ðə 'sekənd 'mi:l əv ðə 'deɪ ɪz 'lʌntʃ, wɪtʃ ðeɪ hæv bɪtwi:n 'twelv ən 'wʌn. 'pi:pl hʊ 'wɜ:k ɪn 'ɒfɪsɪz ən 'fæktərɪz 'ɒfən hæv 'lʌntʃ ɪn ə 'snæk ba: nɪə ðeə 'wɜ:k. ɪt 'dʒenərəlɪ kən'sɪsts əv ə 'sæləd meɪd əv tə'ma:təʊz, 'letɪs ən 'kju:kʌmbə wɪð səm 'kəʊld 'mi:t, ɔ: pə'hæps ə 'tʃi:z 'sænwɪdʒ ən səm 'bɪə.

ɪn ðɪ ˌa:ftə'nu:n, bɪtwi:n 'fɔ:r ən 'faɪv, ðeɪ hæv 'ti: wɪð 'keɪks ɔ: 'θɪn 'slaɪsɪz əv 'bred ən 'bʌtə wɪð 'dʒæm.

ðə 'la:st 'mi:l əv ðə 'deɪ ɪz 'sʌpə, wɪtʃ ɪz 'sɜ:vd ət əbaʊt 'ha:f pa:st 'sɪks. ðen 'ɔ:l ðə 'membəz əv ðə 'fæmɪlɪ 'sɪt tə'geðə. ət 'sʌpə ðeɪ 'i:t 'su:p, 'fɪʃ ɔ: 'mi:t wɪð 'vedʒətəblz, sʌtʃ əz 'pi:z ɔ: ˌfrentʃ 'bi:nz. fə dɪ'zɜ:t ðeɪ 'i:t 'veərɪəs 'kaɪndz əv 'fru:t, sʌtʃ əz bə'na:nəz, 'ɒrɪndʒɪz, 'peəz ɔ:r ə 'pʊdɪŋ.

29
THE MONTHS OF THE YEAR

There are twelve months in a year. The names of the months are:

January, February, March, April, May, June, July, August, September, October, November and December.

Some of them have thirty days, others have thirty-one, and one, February, has twenty-eight days.

There is a little poem to remember how many days each month has:

Thirty days has September,
April, June and November.
All the rest have thirty-one,
Excepting February alone,
Which has but twenty-eight days clear,
And twenty-nine in each leap year.

March, April and May are the spring months. Spring begins on March 21st. June, July and August are the summer months. Summer begins on June 21st. September, October and November are the autumn months. Autumn begins on September 21st. December, January and February are the winter months. Winter begins on December 21st.

The four seasons of the year are:
Spring, summer, autumn and winter.
It is warm in spring. It is hot in summer. It is cool in autumn and it is cold in winter.

autumn otoño	**leap year** año bisiesto	**spring** primavera
cold frío	**months** meses	**summer** verano
cool fresco	**seasons** estaciones	**winter** invierno

29
ðə ˈmʌnθs əv ðə ˈjɪə

ðər ə ˈtwelv ˈmʌnθs ɪn ə ˈjɪə. ðə ˈneɪmz əv ðə ˈmʌnθs ˈɑ: -

ˈdʒænjʊərɪ, ˈfebrʊərɪ, ˈmɑːtʃ, ˈeɪprəl, ˈmeɪ, ˈdʒuːn, dʒʊˈlaɪ, ˈɔːgəst, sepˈtembə, ɒkˈtəubə, nəuˈvembə ən dɪˈsembə.

ˈsʌm əv ðəm hæv ˈθɜːtɪ ˈdeɪz, ˈʌðəz hæv ˌθɜːtɪ ˈwʌn, ən ˈwʌn, ˈfebrʊərɪ, hæz ˈtwentɪ eɪt ˈdeɪz.

ðər ɪz ə ˈlɪtl ˈpəʊɪm tə rɪˈmembə ˈhaʊ menɪ ˈdeɪz ˈiːtʃ ˈmʌnθ ˈhæz :-
ˈθɜːtɪ ˈdeɪz hæz sepˈtembə,
ˈeɪprəl, ˈdʒuːn ən nəʊˈvembə.
ˈɔːl ðə ˈrest hæv ˌθɜːtɪ ˈwʌn,
ɪkˈseptɪŋ ˈfebrʊərɪ əˈləʊn,
wɪtʃ hæz bət ˈtwentɪ eɪt ˈdeɪz ˈklɪə,
ən ˌtwentɪ ˈnaɪn ɪn ˈiːtʃ ˈliːp jɪə.

ˈmɑːtʃ, ˈeɪprəl ən ˈmeɪ ə ðə ˈsprɪŋ ˈmʌnθs. ˈsprɪŋ bɪˈgɪnz ən ˈmɑːtʃ ðə ˌtwentɪ ˈfɜːst. ˈdʒuːn, dʒʊˈlaɪ ənd ˈɔːgəst ə ðə ˈsʌmə ˈmʌnθs. ˈsʌmə bɪˈgɪnz ɒn ˈdʒuːn ðə ˌtwentɪ ˈfɜːst. sepˈtembə, ɒkˈtəubə ən nəʊˈvembə ə ðɪ ˈɔːtəm ˈmʌnθs. ˈɔːtəm bɪˈgɪnz ən sepˈtembə ðə ˌtwentɪ ˈfɜːst. dɪˈsembə ˈdʒænjʊərɪ ən ˈfebrʊərɪ ə ðə ˈwɪntə ˈmʌnθs. ˈwɪntə bɪˈgɪnz ən dɪˈsembə ðə ˌtwentɪ ˈfɜːst.

ðə ˈfɔː ˈsiːzənz əv ðə ˈjɪə ˈɑ: -
ˈsprɪŋ, ˈsʌmə, ˈɔːtəm ən ˈwɪntə.
ɪt ɪz ˈwɔːm ɪn ˈsprɪŋ. ɪt ɪz ˈhɒt ɪn ˈsʌmə. ɪt ɪz ˈkuːl ɪn ˈɔːtəm ənd ɪt ɪz ˈkəʊld ɪn ˈwɪntə.

30
A PARTY

Yesterday, Philip and Muriel had a party because they wanted to celebrate the birth of their first child. The party was a success. Most of their friends came to see the new-born baby. The sitting-room was not large enough for all of them.

They drank wine, orange juice, coke and spirits, such as brandy, gin and whisky. Philip only drank orange juice, as spirits do not agree with him. Muriel offered drinks to her guests. Everybody had a glass in their hand. They talked about a lot of things: traffic, inflation, pollution and many other topics.

At nine o'clock, the guests began to leave the party. As they left, they said to Philip and Muriel:

- Congratulations on the birth of the baby.
- Thank you for a nice party.

When everybody had left the party, the sitting-room was full of half-empty glasses and empty bottles. Philip was very happy, but Muriel was thinking that she had to do the cleaning-up!

birth nacimiento
child niño
cleaning-up limpieza
coke coca-cola

empty vacío
enough bastante
full lleno
guests invitados

juice jugo
new-born recién nacido
spirits licores
success éxito

Congratulations on the birth of the baby Enhorabuena por el nacimiento del niño.

30

ə ˈpɑːtɪ

ˈjestədɪ, ˈfɪlɪp ən ˈmjʊrɪəl hæd ə ˈpɑːtɪ bɪkɒz ðeɪ ˈwɒntɪd
tə ˈselɪbreɪt ðə ˈbɜːθ əv ðeə ˈfɜːst ˈtʃaɪld. ðə ˈpɑːtɪ wəz ə
sək'ses. ˈməʊst əv ðeə ˈfrendz ˈkeɪm tə ˈsiː ðə ˈnjuːbɔːn
ˈbeɪbɪ. ðə ˈsɪtɪŋˌrʊm wəz ˈnɒt ˈlɑːdʒ ɪnʌf fər ˈɔːl əv ðəm.

ðeɪ ˈdræŋk ˈwaɪn, ˈɒrɪndʒ ˌdʒuːs, ˈkəʊk ən ˈspɪrɪts, sʌtʃ əz
ˈbrændɪ, ˈdʒɪn ən ˈwɪskɪ. ˈfɪlɪp ˈəʊnlɪ ˈdræŋk ˈɒrɪndʒ ˌdʒuːs,
əz ˈspɪrɪts dʊ ˈnɒt əˈgriː wɪð hɪm. ˈmjʊrɪəl ˈɒfəd ˈdrɪŋks
tə hə ˈgests. ˈevrɪˌbɒdɪ hæd ə ˈglɑːs ɪn ðeə ˈhænd. ðeɪ ˈtɔːkt
əbaʊt ə ˈlɒt əv ˈθɪŋz :- ˈtræfɪk, ɪnˈfleɪʃən, pəˈluːʃən ənd
ˈmenɪ ʌðə ˈtɒpɪks.

ət ˈnaɪn əklɒk, ðə ˈgests bɪˈgæn tə ˈliːv ðə ˈpɑːtɪ. əz ðeɪ
ˈleft, ðeɪ ˈsed tə ˈfɪlɪp ən ˈmjʊrɪəl :-

- kənˌgrætjʊˈleɪʃənz ɒn ðə ˈbɜːθ əv ðə ˈbeɪbɪ.
- ˈθæŋk jʊ fər ə ˈnaɪs ˈpɑːtɪ.

wen ˈevrɪˌbɒdɪ həd ˈleft ðə ˈpɑːtɪ, ðə ˈsɪtɪŋˌrʊm wəz ˈfʊl əv
ˈhɑːf emtɪ ˈglɑːsɪz ənd ˈemtɪ ˈbɒtlz. ˈfɪlɪp wəz ˈverɪ ˈhæpɪ,
bət ˈmjʊrɪəl wəz ˈθɪŋkɪŋ ðət ʃɪ ˈhæd tə ˈduː ðə ˈkliːnɪŋˈʌp!

31
PETS

A pet is an animal that we keep as a companion and treat with affection. A pet can be a dog, a cat, a bird or a hamster, although some people have very surprising and unusual pets, such as snakes or lizards.

Many families have a pet. It is very nice to have an animal as a companion.

A dog is always faithful to us, but it must be well-fed and needs a lot of looking-after, which takes up a lot of time.

Another very important consideration when keeping a dog, especially in a town, is that it must not be a nuisance to your neighbours.

Some rich people in England become so fond of their pets that they leave their fortunes to them when they die.

bother molestar	**lizard** lagarto	**pet** animal de compañía
faithful fiel	**looking-after** cuidado	**snake** serpiente
fed alimentado	**neighbours** vecinos	**treat** tratar

Become so fond of their pets Quieren tanto a sus animales.

31
ˈpets

ə ˈpet ɪz ən ˈænɪməl ðət wɪ ˈkiːp əz ə kəmˈpænɪən ən ˈtriːt wɪð əˈfekʃən. ə ˈpet kən bɪ ə ˈdɒg, ə ˈkæt, ə ˈbɜːd ɔːr ə ˈhæmstə, ɔːlðəʊ ˈsʌm ˈpiːpl hæv ˈverɪ səˈpraɪzɪŋ ənd ʌnˈjuːʒʊəl ˈpets, sʌtʃ əz ˈsneɪks ɔː ˈlɪzədz.

ˈmenɪ ˈfæmɪlɪz hæv ə ˈpet. ɪt ɪz ˈverɪ ˈnaɪs tə hæv ən ˈænɪməl əz ə kəmˈpænɪən.

ə ˈdɒg ɪz ˈɔːlwɪz ˈfeɪθfəl tʊ əs, bət ɪt məs bɪ ˈwel ˈfed ən ˈniːdz ə ˈlɒt əv ˈlʊkɪŋˈɑːftə, wɪtʃ ˈteɪks ʌp ə ˈlɒt əv ˈtaɪm.

əˈnʌðə ˈverɪ ɪmˈpɔːtənt kənˌsɪdəˈreɪʃən wen ˈkiːpɪŋ ə ˈdɒg, ɪsˈpeʃəlɪ ɪn ə ˈtaʊn, ɪz ðət ɪt məs ˈnɒt bɪ ə ˈnjuːsəns tə jɔː ˈneɪbəz.

ˈsʌm ˈrɪtʃ ˈpiːpl ɪn ˈɪŋglənd bɪˈkʌm ˈsəʊ ˈfɒnd əv ðeə ˈpets ðət ðeɪ ˈliːv ðeə ˈfɔːtʃənz tə ðəm wen ðeɪ ˈdaɪ.

32
A PICNIC

It is a warm morning in August. The Browns have just decided to go for a picnic and Mrs Brown is getting the picnic basket ready. Mr Brown is helping her.

- Have you put the plates and the glasses in the basket?
- No, I haven't put them in yet. They are on the kitchen table. Bring them, please.
- Don't forget the forks and the knives.
- No, I won't forget them.
- Where are the sandwiches?
- Mavis is preparing them.
- I'll put the wine and the fruit in this bag.
- Listen, I'll do this if you like. Why don't you go and get the car out of the garage?
- Okay.

An hour later, they are in the country. At last they have found a suitable tree and Mrs Brown is spreading a table-cloth on the grass. Mavis and Peggy are helping her take everything out of the basket. They have just had lunch and now they are resting. The girls' father is sitting on a folding chair, reading the newspaper and their mother is knitting. Peggy and Mavis are trying to catch butterflies. At about four, some clouds begin to hide the sun. Then Mrs Brown says:

- It's getting a bit cool. Let's go back home.

Then they all collect everything they have spread on the grass leaving no litter behind, get into the car and go back home.

collect recoger	**litter** basura	**spread** extender,
knit hacer punto	**shine** brillar	extendido

32

ə ˈpɪknɪk

ɪt ɪz ə ˈwɔːm ˈmɔːnɪŋ ɪn ˈɔːgəst. ðə ˈbraʊnz həv ˈdʒʌst dɪˈsaɪdɪd tə ˈgəʊ fər ə ˈpɪknɪk ənd mɪsɪz ˈbraʊn ɪz ˈgetɪŋ ðə ˈpɪknɪk ˌbɑːskɪt ˈredɪ. mɪstə ˈbraʊn ɪz ˈhelpɪŋ hə.

- həv jʊ ˈpʊt ðə ˈpleɪts ən ðə ˈglɑːsɪz ɪn ðə ˈbɑːskɪt?
- ˈnəʊ, aɪ ˈhævənt pʊt ðəm ˈɪn jet. ðeɪ ər ɒn ðə ˌkɪtʃən ˈteɪbl.
  ˈbrɪŋ ðəm, ˈpliːz.
- ˈdəʊnt fəˈget ðə ˈfɔːks ən ðə ˈnaɪvz.
- ˈnəʊ, aɪ ˈwəʊnt fəˈget ðəm.
- ˈweər ə ðə ˈsænwɪdʒɪz?
- ˈmeɪvɪs ɪz prɪˈpeərɪŋ ðəm.
- aɪl ˈpʊt ðə ˈwaɪn ən ðə ˈfruːt ɪn ðɪs ˈbæg.
- ˈlɪsən, aɪl ˈduː: ˈðɪs ɪf jʊ ˈlaɪk. ˈwaɪ dəʊnt jʊ ˈgəʊ ən ˈget ðə ˈkɑːr aʊt əv ðə ˈgærɑːʒ?
- ˈəʊˈkeɪ.

ən ˈaʊə ˈleɪtə, ðeɪ ər ɪn ðə ˈkʌntrɪ. ət ˈlɑːst ðeɪ həv ˈfaʊnd ə ˈsuːtəbl ˈtriː ən mɪsɪz ˈbraʊn ɪz ˈspredɪŋ ə ˈteɪblklɒθ ɒn ðə ˈgrɑːs. ˈmeɪvɪs ən ˈpegɪ ə ˈhelpɪŋ hə ˈteɪk ˈevrɪθɪŋ aʊt əv ðə ˈbɑːskɪt. ðeɪ həv ˈdʒʌst hæd ˈlʌntʃ ən ˈnaʊ ðeɪ ə ˈrestɪŋ. ðə ˈgɜːlz ˈfɑːðə ɪz ˈsɪtɪŋ ɒn ə ˈfəʊldɪŋ ˈtʃeə, ˈriːdɪŋ ðə ˈnjuːsˌpeɪpə ən ðeə ˈmʌðə ɪz ˈnɪtɪŋ. ˈpegɪ ən ˈmeɪvɪs ə ˈtraɪɪŋ tə ˈkætʃ ˈbʌtəflaɪz. ət əˈbaʊt ˈfɔː, səm ˈklaʊdz bɪˈgɪn tə ˈhaɪd ðə ˈsʌn. ðen mɪsɪz ˈbraʊn ˈsez :-

- ɪts ˈgetɪŋ ə ˈbɪt ˈkuːl. ˈlets gəʊ ˈbæk ˈhəʊm.

ðen ðeɪ ˈɔːl kəˈlekt ˈevrɪθɪŋ ðeɪ həv ˈspred ɒn ðə ˈgrɑːs ˈliːvɪŋ ˈnəʊ ˈlɪtə bɪˈhaɪnd, ˈget ɪntə ðə ˈkɑː ən ˈgəʊ bæk ˈhəʊm.

33
ON A PLANE

I'm on a plane now. I'm flying to London. I'm in tourist class. The plane is full of people from different countries. The air-hostess is serving lunch.

The view from the plane is wonderful. Below I can see fields, villages, rivers and mountains, as if it were a map. Now the plane is flying above the sea. There are some ships on the sea. There, in front of me, is the English coast.

At this moment, the loud-speakers are announcing that we are about to land. Now we are landing and I can feel the wheels of the plane touching the ground. The plane has stopped and the passengers are getting out. Now we have to pass through Customs. I can see my English friends waiting for me, and they ask me:

- Did you like the flight?
- Yes, I liked it very much. It was wonderful.

air-hostess azafata	**get out** salir	**ships** barcos
announce anunciar	**ground** tierra	**touch** tocar
coast costa	**land** aterrizar	**view** vista
Customs Aduana	**loud-speakers** altavoces	**village** pueblo
flight vuelo	**map** mapa	**wheels** ruedas
fly volar	**passengers** pasajeros	**wonderful** maravilloso

We are about to land Estamos a punto de aterrizar.

33
ɒn ə 'pleɪn

aɪm ɒn ə 'pleɪn 'naʊ. aɪm 'flaɪɪŋ tə 'lʌndən. aɪm ɪn 'tʊərɪst ˌklɑːs. ðə 'pleɪn ɪz 'fʊl əv 'piːpl frəm 'dɪfərənt 'kʌntrɪz. ðɪ 'eəˌhɒstɪs ɪz 'sɜːvɪŋ 'lʌntʃ.

ðə 'vjuː frəm ðə 'pleɪn ɪz 'wʌndəfəl. bɪ'ləʊ aɪ kən 'siː 'fiːldz, 'vɪlɪdʒɪz, 'rɪvəz ən 'maʊntənz, əz ɪf ɪt wər ə 'mæp. 'naʊ ðə 'pleɪn ɪz 'flaɪɪŋ əbʌv ðə 'siː. ðər ə səm 'ʃɪps ɒn ðə 'siː. 'ðeə, ɪn 'frʌnt əv mɪ, ɪz ðɪ 'ɪŋglɪʃ 'kəʊst.

ət ðɪs 'məʊmənt, ðə ˌlaʊd'spiːkəz ər ə'naʊnsɪŋ ðət wɪ ər əbaʊt tə 'lænd. 'naʊ wɪ ə 'lændɪŋ ənd aɪ kən 'fiːl ðə 'wiːlz əv ðə 'pleɪn 'tʌtʃɪŋ ðə 'graʊnd. ðə 'pleɪn həz 'stɒpt ən ðə 'pæsɪndʒəz ə 'getɪŋ 'aʊt. 'naʊ wɪ 'hæv tə 'pɑːs θruː 'kʌstəmz. aɪ kən 'siː maɪ 'ɪŋglɪʃ 'frendz 'weɪtɪŋ fə mɪ, ən ðeɪ 'ɑːsk mɪ :-

- dɪd jʊ 'laɪk ðə 'flaɪt?
- 'jes, aɪ laɪkt ɪt 'verɪ 'mʌtʃ. ɪt wəz 'wʌndəfəl.

34

IN THE PLAYGROUND

It is playtime. The children are in their school playground.

Peter and John are running around a tree. Peter is running after John.

There are some boys near the wall in the corner. They are playing marbles. Bruce, Tom and Jim are rolling their marbles along the ground. Some other boys are standing around them watching the game.

Several boys are playing football in the middle of the playground. Robert has just kicked the ball to Tony. Now the ball is rolling along the ground and all the boys are running after it.

In a corner of the playground, there are some girls with a skipping-rope. Near them, two girls and three boys are playing hide-and-seek. It is a game in which some children hide and others try to find them.

Near the school door, Philip, Steve and Patrick are playing leapfrog. It is a game in which one player jumps over the others, who stand with their backs bent.

At this moment, the bell rings and all the children have to stop playing. They must go back to class.

around alrededor	**jump** saltar	**roll** rodar
ball pelota	**kick** dar una patada	**run** correr
bent encorvadas	**leapfrog** pídola	**skipping-rope** comba
corner rincón	**marbles** canicas	**stand** estar de pie
find encontrar	**player** jugador	**standing** de pie
go back volver	**playground** patio de	**try** tratar
hide-and-seek escondite	recreo	**wall** pared, muro

34
ɪn ðə 'pleɪɡraʊnd

ɪts 'pleɪtaɪm. ðə 'tʃɪldrən ər ɪn ðeə 'sku:l ˌpleɪɡraʊnd.

'pi:tər ən 'dʒɒn ə 'rʌnɪŋ əraʊnd ə 'tri:. 'pi:tər ɪz 'rʌnɪŋ ɑ:ftə 'dʒɒn.

ðər ə səm 'bɔɪz nɪə ðə 'wɔ:l ɪn ðə 'kɔ:nə. ðeɪ ə 'pleɪɪŋ 'mɑ:blz. 'bru:s, 'tɒm ən 'dʒɪm ə 'rəʊlɪŋ ðeə 'mɑ:blz əlɒŋ ðə 'graʊnd. 'sʌm ʌðə 'bɔɪz ə 'stændɪŋ ə'raʊnd ðəm 'wɒtʃɪŋ ðə 'ɡeɪm.

'sevərəl 'bɔɪz ə 'pleɪɪŋ 'fʊtbɔ:l ɪn ðə 'mɪdl əv ðə 'pleɪɡraʊnd. 'rɒbət həz dʒʌst 'kɪkt ðə 'bɔ:l tə 'təʊnɪ. naʊ ðə 'bɔ:l ɪz 'rəʊlɪŋ əlɒŋ ðə 'graʊnd ənd 'ɔ:l ðə 'bɔɪz ə 'rʌnɪŋ 'ɑ:ftər ɪt.

ɪn ə 'kɔ:nər əv ðə 'pleɪɡraʊnd, ðər ə səm 'ɡɜ:lz wɪð ə 'skɪpɪŋ ˌrəʊp. 'nɪə ðəm, 'tu: 'ɡɜ:lz ən 'θri: bɔɪz ə 'pleɪɪŋ ˌhaɪdən'si:k. ɪt ɪz ə 'ɡeɪm ɪn wɪtʃ səm 'tʃɪldrən 'haɪd ən 'ʌðəz 'traɪ tə 'faɪnd ðəm.

nɪə ðə 'sku:l dɔ:, 'fɪlɪp, 'sti:v ən 'pætrɪk ə 'pleɪɪŋ 'li:pfrɒɡ. ɪt ɪz ə 'ɡeɪm ɪn wɪtʃ 'wʌn 'pleɪə 'dʒʌmps əʊvə ðɪ 'ʌðəz, hʊ 'stænd wɪð ðeə 'bæks 'bent.

ət ðɪs 'məʊmənt, ðə 'bel 'rɪŋz ənd 'ɔ:l ðə 'tʃɪldrən 'hæv tə 'stɒp 'pleɪɪŋ. ðeɪ məs 'ɡəʊ 'bæk tə 'klɑ:s.

35
AT THE POST OFFICE

You go to the post office when you want to register a letter or send a parcel. You do not need to go to the post office when you just want to send a letter because you can post it in any pillar-box. In England, you buy stamps at post offices, not at tobacconists' as in Spain.

In a post office the clerks are usually very busy. If you want to register a letter, you ask the clerk for a form which you have to fill in. Then you hand it to him, and he writes something on it. Then he gives you a slip of paper. He also gives you a stamp or two which you stick in the top right-hand corner of the envelope.

Here is a conversation between a lady and the clerk at the post office:

- How much does it cost to send a letter to New York, please?
- Twelve pence if it isn't more than two ounces.
- I want to send a money order to Rome.
- Fill in this form and go to that counter over there.
- Thank you.

There is a queue at the counter. The lady waits for a while. When her turn comes, she hands the money together with the form to the clerk, who gives her a slip of paper. Then she walks out of the post office.

counter mostrador	**money order** giro	**send** enviar
envelope sobre	**parcel** paquete	**stamps** sellos
fill in rellenar	**pillar-box** buzón	**stick** pegar
form impreso	**post** echar al correo	**tobacconists'** estancos
hand entregar	**queue** cola (fila)	**turn** turno
letter carta	**register** certificar	**usually** normalmente

35
ət ðə ˈpəʊst ˌɒfɪs

juː ˈɡəʊ tə ðə ˈpəʊst ˌɒfɪs wen juː ˈwɒnt tə ˈredʒɪstə ə ˈletə ɔː ˈsend ə ˈpɑːsl. juː duː ˈnɒt ˈniːd tə ˈɡəʊ tə ðə ˈpəʊst ˌɒfɪs wen juː ˈdʒʌst ˈwɒnt tə ˈsend ə ˈletə bɪkɒz juː kən ˈpəʊst ɪt ɪn enɪ ˈpɪləbɒks. ɪn ˈɪŋɡlənd, juː ˈbaɪ ˈstæmps ət ˈpəʊst ˌɒfɪsɪz, ˈnɒt ət təˈbækənɪsts əz ɪn ˈspeɪn.

ɪn ə ˈpəʊst ˌɒfɪs ðə ˈklɑːks ə ˈjuːʒʊəlɪ verɪ ˈbɪzɪ. ɪf juː ˈwɒnt tə ˈredʒɪstər ə ˈletə, juː ˈɑːsk ðə ˈklɑːk fər ə ˈfɔːm wɪtʃ juː ˈhæv tə ˈfɪl ˈɪn. ðen juː ˈhænd ɪt tə hɪm, ən hɪ ˈraɪts ˈsʌmθɪŋ ɒn ɪt. ðen hɪ ˈɡɪvz juː ə ˈslɪp əv ˈpeɪpə. hɪ ˈɔːlsəʊ ˈɡɪvz juː ə ˈstæmp ɔː ˈtuː wɪtʃ juː ˈstɪk ɪn ðə ˈtɒp ˈraɪt hænd ˈkɔːnər əv ðɪ ˈenvələʊp.

ˈhɪər ɪz ə ˌkɒnvəˈseɪʃən bɪtwiːn ə ˈleɪdɪ ən ðə ˈklɑːk ət ðə ˈpəʊst ˌɒfɪs :-

- ˈhaʊ ˈmʌtʃ dəz ɪt ˈkɒst tə ˈsend ə ˈletə tə ˌnjuː ˈjɔːk, ˈpliːz?
- ˈtwelv ˈpens ɪf ɪt ˈɪzənt ˈmɔː ðən ˈtuː ˈaʊnsɪz.
- aɪ ˈwɒnt tə ˈsend ə ˈmʌnɪ ˌɔːdə tə ˈrəʊm.
- ˈfɪl ˈɪn ðɪs ˈfɔːm ən ˈɡəʊ tə ðæt ˈkaʊntə əʊvə ˈðeə.
- ˈθæŋk juː.

ðər ɪz ə ˈkjuː ət ðə ˈkaʊntə. ðə ˈleɪdɪ ˈweɪts fər ə ˈwaɪl. wen hə ˈtɜːn ˈkʌmz, ʃɪ ˈhændz ðə ˈmʌnɪ təˈɡeðə wɪð ðə ˈfɔːm tə ðə ˈklɑːk, hʊ ˈɡɪvz hər ə ˈslɪp əv ˈpeɪpə. ðen ʃɪ ˈwɔːks aʊt əv ðə ˈpəʊst ˌɒfɪs.

36
AT THE RESTAURANT

A restaurant is a place where meals can be bought and eaten. When you go into a restaurant and sit down at a table, a waiter or sometimes a waitress comes and hands you the menu. You read it carefully and choose the dish you like best. Then you call the waiter and order the dishes you have chosen. Here is a conversation between a customer and the waiter:
- Good afternoon, sir.
- Good afternoon. May I have the menu, please?
- Certainly, sir.

The customer reads the menu: "Meat, fish, soup, salad, poached eggs, roast beef."
- I'll have some soup followed by roast beef with vegetables. For dessert, I would like apple pie, please.
- Anything to drink, sir?
- I'll have some wine and mineral water, please.

After the customer has eaten his dinner, he calls the waiter again and asks him:
- Can I have the bill, please?

The waiter goes away and, a few minutes later, he comes back with the bill and says:
- Here it is, sir.

Then the man leaves the money on the table together with a tip for the waiter. He puts on his coat and walks out of the restaurant.

bill nota (factura)	**customer** cliente	**pie** pastel
carefully con cuidado	**eaten** comido	**poached** escalfados
chosen elegido	**followed** seguido	**tip** propina
come back volver	**go away** irse	**together with** junto con

74

36

ət ðə 'restərənt

ə 'restərənt ɪz ə pleɪs weə 'mi:lz kən bɪ 'bɔ:t ən 'i:tən. wen ju 'gəu ɪntu ə 'restərənt ən 'sɪt 'daun ət ə 'teɪbl, ə 'weɪtə ɔ: 'sʌmtaɪmz ə 'weɪtrɪs 'kʌmz ən 'hændz ju ðə 'menju. ju 'ri:d ɪt 'keəfəlɪ ən 'tʃu:z ðə 'dɪʃ ju 'laɪk 'best. ðen ju 'kɔ:l ðə 'weɪtə ənd 'ɔ:də ðə 'dɪʃɪz ju həv 'tʃəuzən. 'hɪər ɪz ə ˌkɒnvə'seɪʃn bɪtwi:n ə 'kʌstəmə ən ðə 'weɪtə :-
- gud ˌɑ:ftə'nu:n, sə.
- gud ˌɑ:ftə'nu:n. meɪ aɪ hæv ðə 'menju, 'pli:z?
- 'sɜ:tənlɪ, sə.

ðə 'kʌstəmə 'ridz ðə 'menju :- 'mi:t, 'fɪʃ, 'su:p, 'sæləd, 'pəutʃt 'egz, 'rəust 'bi:f.
- aɪl hæv səm 'su:p 'fɒləud baɪ 'rəust 'bi:f wɪð 'vedʒətəblz. fə dɪ'zɜ:t, aɪ wəd 'laɪk ˌæpl 'paɪ, 'pli:z.
- 'enɪθɪŋ tə 'drɪŋk, sə?
- aɪl hæv səm 'waɪn ən 'mɪnərəl 'wɔ:tə, 'pli:z.

ɑ:ftə ðə 'kʌstəmə həz 'i:tən hɪz 'dɪnə, hi 'kɔ:lz ðə 'weɪtə ə'geɪn ənd 'ɑ:sks hɪm :-
- kən aɪ hæv ðə 'bɪl, 'pli:z?

ðə 'weɪtə 'gəuz ə'weɪ ənd, ə 'fju: mɪnɪts 'leɪtə, hi 'kʌmz 'bæk wɪð ðə 'bɪl ən 'sez :-
- 'hɪər ɪt 'ɪz, sə.

ðen ðə 'mæn 'li:vz ðə 'mʌnɪ ɒn ðə 'teɪbl tə'geðə wɪð ə 'tɪp fə ðə 'weɪtə. hi 'puts ɒn hɪz 'kəut ən 'wɔ:ks aut əv ðə 'restərənt.

37
AT THE SEASIDE

Last week, the Martins went to Benidorm. They stayed at the Park Hotel, which is near the beach.

The weather was very good. The sun shone brightly all the time.

As soon as they arrived at the hotel, they put on their bathing suits and went to the beach. They sunbathed and had a swim in the sea. The water was warm.

On Saturday morning, they rented a beach umbrella, as the sun was very strong. They sat under the umbrella and Mr Martin helped his children make a sandcastle with turrets and a drawbridge.

In the afternoon, they went for a walk along the promenade, which was full of tourists from many countries.

On Sunday morning, they had another swim in the sea, and in the afternoon they came back to Madrid.

bathing suits trajes de baño
beach playa
brightly brillantemente
castle castillo
drawbridge puente levadizo

promenade paseo marítimo
rented alquilaron
sand arena
sat se sentaron
shone brilló
stay hospedarse

strong fuerte
sunbathe tomar el sol
swim nadar, baño
turrets torreones
umbrella sombrilla
walk paseo
weather tiempo

They had a swim in the sea Nadaron en el mar.

37

ət ðə 'si:said

'la:st 'wi:k, ðə 'ma:tɪnz 'went tə ˌbenɪ'dɒrm. ðeɪ 'steɪd ət ðə 'pa:k həʊ'tel, wɪtʃ ɪz nɪə ðə 'bi:tʃ.

ðə 'weðə wəz verɪ 'gʊd. ðə 'sʌn 'ʃɒn 'braɪtlɪ 'ɔ:l ðə 'taɪm.

əz 'su:n əz ðeɪ ə'raɪvd ət ðə həʊ'tel, ðeɪ 'pʊt ɒn ðeə 'beɪðɪŋ ˌsu:ts ən 'went tə ðə 'bi:tʃ. ðeɪ 'sʌnbeɪðd ən hæd ə 'swɪm ɪn ðə 'si:. ðə 'wɔ:tə wəz 'wɔ:m.

ɒn 'sætədɪ 'mɔ:nɪŋ, ðeɪ 'rentɪd ə 'bi:tʃ ʌmˌbrelə, əz ðə 'sʌn wəz verɪ 'strɒŋ. ðeɪ 'sæt ʌndə ðɪ ʌm'brelə ən mɪstə 'ma:tɪn 'helpt hɪz 'tʃɪldrən meɪk ə 'sændka:sl wɪð 'tʌrɪts ənd ə 'drɔ:brɪdʒ.

ɪn ðɪ ˌa:ftə'nu:n, ðeɪ 'went fər ə 'wɔ:k əlɒŋ ðə ˌprɒmə'na:d, wɪtʃ wəz 'fʊl əv 'tʊərɪsts frəm 'menɪ 'kʌntrɪz.

ɒn 'sʌndɪ 'mɔ:nɪŋ, ðeɪ hæd ə'nʌðə 'swɪm ɪn ðə 'si:, ənd ɪn ðɪ ˌa:ftə'nu:n ðeɪ 'keɪm 'bæk tə mə'drɪd.

38
SHAPES

Round, square, rectangular and oval are shapes. A plate is round; a handkerchief is square; a picture frame is rectangular; an egg is oval.

This is a box. It's as long as it is broad.
- What shape is it? - It's square.

This is another box. It's longer than it is broad. It isn't square.
- What shape is it? - It's rectangular.

This is a plate.
- What shape is it? - It's round.

This is a dish. It isn't round like a plate.
- What shape is it? - It's oval.

Look at the things around you and answer these questions:
- What shape is this room?
- What shape is your ring?
- What shape is your watch?
- What shape is this table?
- What shape is your mirror?
- What shape is your television set?

around alrededor	**long** largo	**ring** anillo
broad ancho	**longer** más largo	**round** redondo
dish fuente (plato)	**mirror** espejo	**shape** forma
frame marco	**oval** ovalado	**square** cuadrado
handkerchief pañuelo	**picture** cuadro	**watch** reloj

38
'ʃeɪps

'raʊnd, 'skweə, rekˈtæŋgjʊlə ənd 'əʊvəl ə 'ʃeɪps. ə 'pleɪt ɪz 'raʊnd; ə 'hæŋkətʃɪf ɪz 'skweə; ə 'pɪktʃə ˌfreɪm ɪz rekˈtæŋgjʊlə; ən 'eg ɪz 'əʊvəl.

'ðɪs ɪz ə 'bɒks. ɪts əz 'lɒŋ əz ɪt ɪz 'brɔːd.
- wɒt 'ʃeɪp ɪz ɪt? - ɪts 'skweə.

'ðɪs ɪz əˈnʌðə bɒks. ɪts 'lɒŋgə ðən ɪts 'brɔːd. ɪt 'ɪzənt 'skweə.
- wɒt 'ʃeɪp ɪz ɪt? - ɪts rekˈtæŋgjʊlə.

'ðɪs ɪz ə 'pleɪt.
- wɒt 'ʃeɪp ɪz ɪt? - ɪts 'raʊnd.

'ðɪs ɪz ə 'dɪʃ. ɪt 'ɪzənt 'raʊnd laɪk ə 'pleɪt.
- wɒt 'ʃeɪp ɪz ɪt? - ɪts 'əʊvəl.

'lʊk ət ðə 'θɪŋz əˈraʊnd jʊ ənd 'ɑːnsə ðiːz 'kwestʃənz :-
- wɒt 'ʃeɪp ɪz ðɪs 'rʊm?
- wɒt 'ʃeɪp ɪz jɔː 'rɪŋ?
- wɒt 'ʃeɪp ɪz jɔː 'wɒtʃ?
- wɒt 'ʃeɪp ɪz ðɪs 'teɪbl?
- wɒt 'ʃeɪp ɪz jɔː 'mɪrə?
- wɒt 'ʃeɪp ɪz jɔː 'telɪvɪʒən ˌset?

39
SHOPS

In the street where I live, there are many shops. When I walk from my house to the underground station, I like looking in the shop windows.

There's a grocer's shop with lots of good things, such as pots of jam, and tins of biscuits. Then comes a greengrocer's. He has vegetables, such as carrots, cabbages, cauliflowers and onions, in one half of the shop and in the other half, you can see all kinds of fruit, such as pears, oranges, bananas and grapes.

I like looking in a toy shop which is near. There you can see a lot of toys: footballs, toy cars and toy planes. When I go with my sister, she looks at the dolls and teddy bears. Near the bank, there's a furniture shop and next to it, there's a chemist's. My mother always buys medicine there.

On the other side of the street, there's a jeweller's, a large shoe-shop and a bookseller's, where my father sometimes buys books. Near the underground station, there's a stationer's, where I buy all I need for school: pencils, rubbers, notebooks and rulers.

biscuits galletas
bookseller's librería
cabbages coles
cauliflowers coliflores
chemist's farmacia
greengrocer's verdulería
grocer's tienda de comestibles

jeweller's joyería
notebooks cuadernos
onions cebollas
pencils lápices
pots tarros
rubbers gomas de borrar
rulers reglas
shoe-shop zapatería

shop tienda
shop window escaparate
stationer's papelería
teddy bear osito de trapo
toy shop juguetería
underground station estación de metro

39
'ʃɒps

ɪn ðə 'striːt weər aɪ 'lɪv, ðər ə 'menɪ 'ʃɒps. wen aɪ 'wɔːk
frəm maɪ 'haʊs tə ðɪ 'ʌndəgraʊnd 'steɪʃən, aɪ 'laɪk 'lʊkɪŋ ɪn
ðə ʃɒp 'wɪndəʊz.

ðəz ə 'grəʊsəz ʃɒp wɪð 'lɒts əv 'gʊd 'θɪŋz, sʌtʃ əz 'pɒts əv
'dʒæm ən 'tɪnz əv 'bɪskɪts. ðen 'kʌmz ə 'griːŋgrəʊsəz. hɪ
hæz 'vedʒətəblz, sʌtʃ əz 'kærəts, 'kæbɪdʒɪz, 'kɒlɪˌflaʊəz ənd
'ʌnjənz, ɪn 'wʌn 'haːf əv ðə 'ʃɒp ənd ɪn ðɪ 'ʌðə haːf, jʊ kən
'siː: 'ɔːl 'kaɪndz əv 'fruːt, sʌtʃ əz 'peəz, 'ɒrɪndʒɪz, bə'naːnəz
ən 'greɪps.

aɪ 'laɪk 'lʊkɪŋ ɪn ə 'tɔɪ ʃɒp wɪtʃ ɪz 'nɪə. 'ðeə jʊ kən 'siː: ə 'lɒt
əv 'tɔɪz :- 'fʊtbɔːlz, 'tɔɪ kaːz ən 'tɔɪ pleɪnz. wen aɪ 'gəʊ wɪð
maɪ 'sɪstə, ʃɪ 'lʊks ət ðə 'dɒlz ən 'tedɪ ˌbeəz. 'nɪə ðə 'bæŋk,
ðəz ə 'fɜːnɪtʃə ʃɒp ən 'nekst tʊ ɪt, ðəz ə 'kemɪsts. maɪ 'mʌðə
'ɔːlwɪz 'baɪz 'medsən ðeə.

ɒn ðɪ 'ʌðə 'saɪd əv ðə 'striːt, ðəz ə 'dʒuːələz, ə 'laːdʒ 'ʃuːʃɒp
ənd ə 'bʊkˌseləz, weə maɪ 'faːðə 'sʌmtaɪmz 'baɪz 'bʊks.
nɪə ðɪ 'ʌndəgraʊnd 'steɪʃən, ðəz ə 'steɪʃənəz, weər aɪ 'baɪ
'ɔːl aɪ 'niːd fə 'skuːl :- 'pensəlz, 'rʌbəz, 'nəʊtbʊks ən 'ruːləz.

40
SPORTS AND GAMES

Skiing, golf, shooting, cycling and swimming are sports. Football, rugby, basketball, baseball and tennis are outdoor games. There are many other games played indoors, which are called indoor games, such as skittles, dominoes, draughts, chess, darts, not to mention the numerous card games.

People practise sports and play games. To become a good sportsman, you must devote a lot of time to training for the sport you like best.

Outdoor games must be played when the weather is good. In the long winter evenings, friends and relatives meet to play indoor games.

Many people like gambling, that is, betting their money on games of chance or skill, but really there is nothing like playing for the sake of playing, regardless of whether you win or lose.

become llegar a ser	**draughts** damas (juego)	**shooting** tiro
cards cartas	**gamble** jugar dinero	**skiing** el esquí
chance suerte	**indoor** bajo techo	**skittles** bolos
chess ajedrez	**lose** perder	**swimming** natación
cycling ciclismo	**outdoor** al aire libre	**train** entrenarse
darts dardos	**play** jugar	**whether** si
devote dedicar	**relatives** parientes	**win** ganar

For the sake of Por el placer de.
Regardless of Sin tener en cuenta.

40
'spɔ:ts ən 'geɪmz

'ski:ɪŋ, 'gɒlf, 'ʃu:tɪŋ, 'saɪklɪŋ ən 'swɪmɪŋ ə 'spɔ:ts. 'fʊtbɔ:l, 'rʌgbɪ, 'ba:skɪtˌbɔ:l, 'beɪsbɔ:l ən 'tenɪs ər 'aʊtdɔ: 'geɪmz. ðər ə 'menɪ ʌðə 'geɪmz 'pleɪd ɪn'dɔ:z, wɪtʃ ə 'kɔ:ld 'ɪndɔ: 'geɪmz, sʌtʃ əz 'skɪtlz, 'dɒmɪnəʊz, 'dra:fts, 'tʃes, 'da:ts, 'nɒt tə 'menʃən ðə 'nju:mərəs 'ka:d geɪmz.

'pi:pl 'præktɪs 'spɔ:ts ən 'pleɪ 'geɪmz. tə br'kʌm ə 'gʊd 'spɔ:tsmən, jʊ məs dɪ'vəʊt ə 'lɒt əv 'taɪm tə 'treɪnɪŋ fə ðə 'spɔ:t jʊ 'laɪk 'best.

'aʊtdɔ: 'geɪmz məs bɪ 'pleɪd wen ðə 'weðər ɪz 'gʊd. ɪn ðə 'lɒŋ 'wɪntə 'i:vnɪŋz, 'frendz ən 'relətɪvz 'mi:t tə 'pleɪ 'ɪndɔ: 'geɪmz.

'menɪ 'pi:pl laɪk 'gæmblɪŋ, 'ðæt ɪs, 'betɪŋ ðeə 'mʌnɪ ɒn 'geɪmz əv 'tʃa:ns ɔ: 'skɪl, bət 'rɪəlɪ ðər ɪz 'nʌθɪŋ laɪk 'pleɪɪŋ fə ðə 'seɪk əv 'pleɪɪŋ, rɪ'ga:dlɪs əv weðə jʊ 'wɪn ɔ: 'lu:z.

41
A STREET

The street where I live is in the centre of the town. It is a very busy street. There are a lot of cars and buses running along it. The traffic is controlled by traffic lights, although there is usually a policeman at the crossroads.

In front of my house, there is a zebra-crossing and a bus stop. There are trees and lampposts along the street. There are houses on each side of the street.

In this street there are a lot of shops, a cinema, a bank, a church and a school. A few yards down the street, there is a square with a fountain in the middle and a little garden round it, where children play on sunny afternoons.

along a lo largo de
although aunque
bus stop parada de autobús
controlled controlado
crossroads cruce
few pocos, pocas
fountain fuente
garden jardín
lampposts farolas
square plaza
sunny soleadas
traffic lights semáforos
zebra-crossing paso de cebra

On sunny afternoons Las tardes soleadas.

41
ə ˈstriːt

ðə ˈstriːt weər aɪ lɪv ɪz ɪn ðə ˈsentər əv ðə ˈtaʊn. ɪt ɪz ə ˈverɪ
bɪzɪ ˈstriːt. ðər ər ə ˈlɒt əv ˈkaːz ən ˈbʌsɪz ˈrʌnɪŋ əˈlɒŋ ɪt. ðə
ˈtræfɪk ɪz kənˈtrəʊld baɪ ˈtræfɪk laɪts, ɔːlðəʊ ðər ɪz ˈjuːʒʊəlɪ ə
pəˈliːsmən ət ðə ˈkrɒsrəʊdz.

ɪn frʌnt əv maɪ ˈhaʊs, ðər ɪz ə ˈzebrəkrɒsɪŋ ənd ə ˈbʌs stɒp.
ðər ə ˈtriːz ən ˈlæmppəʊsts əlɒŋ ðə ˈstriːt. ðər ə ˈtriːz ən ˈhaʊzɪz
ɒn ˈiːtʃ ˈsaɪd əv ðə ˈstriːt.

ɪn ðɪs ˈstriːt ðər ər ə ˈlɒt əv ˈʃɒps, ə ˈsɪnəmə, ə ˈbæŋk, ə ˈtʃɜːtʃ
ənd ə ˈskuːl. ə ˈfjuː ˈjaːdz daʊn ðə ˈstriːt, ðər ɪz ə ˈskweə wɪð
ə ˈfaʊntən ɪn ðə ˈmɪdl ənd ə ˈlɪtl ˈgaːdən ˈraʊnd ɪt, weə ˈtʃɪldrən
ˈpleɪ ɒn ˈsʌnɪ ˌaːftəˈnuːnz.

42

THE TELEPHONE

If you want to make a telephone call, you must lift up the receiver, wait for the dialling tone and dial the number you want.

At this moment, the telephone rings and Peter Jones picks up the receiver:
- Hello!
- Is that you, Peter?
- Yes. Who's speaking?
- It's Bill Andrews speaking.
- Will you speak a bit louder, please? I can't hear you properly.
- Can you hear me now?
- Yes, I can hear you quite well now.
- Peter, I rang up to ask you if you were free this morning. I wonder if I might come and see you to talk to you about a very important matter.
- I'm rather busy this morning. Couldn't you come this afternoon?
- At what time shall I come?
- Come at five o'clock.
- All right. I'll see you at five. Thank you very much.
- Not at all.
- Goodbye, Peter.
- Goodbye, Bill.

call llamada	**lift up** levantar	**receiver** auricular
dial marcar	**number** número	**ring** sonar
dialling tone tono	**pick up** coger	**wait** esperar
hear oír	**properly** debidamente	**wonder** preguntarse

Not at all De nada.
A bit louder Un poco más alto.

42
ðə ˈtelɪfəʊn

ɪf jʊ ˈwɒnt tə ˈmeɪk ə ˈtelɪfəʊn ˌkɔːl, jʊ məs ˈlɪft ʌp ðə rɪˈsiːvə, ˈweɪt fə ðə ˈdaɪəlɪŋ ˌtəʊn ən ˈdaɪəl ðə ˈnʌmbə jʊ ˈwɒnt.

ət ðɪs ˈməʊmənt, ðə ˈtelɪfəʊn ˈrɪŋz ən ˈpiːtə ˈdʒəʊnz ˈpɪks ʌp ðə rɪˈsiːvə :-

- həˈləʊ!
- ɪz ˈðæt ˈjuː, ˈpiːtə?
- ˈjes. ˈhuːz ˈspiːkɪŋ?
- ɪts ˈbɪl ˈændruːz spiːkɪŋ.
- wɪl jʊ ˈspiːk ə ˈbɪt ˈlaʊdə, ˈpliːz? aɪ ˈkɑːnt hɪə jʊ ˈprɒpəlɪ.
- kən jʊ ˈhɪə mɪ ˈnaʊ?
- jes, aɪ kən hɪə jʊ ˈkwaɪt ˈwel ˈnaʊ.
- ˈpiːtə, aɪ ˈræŋ ʌp tʊ ˈɑːsk jʊ ɪf jʊ wə ˈfriː ðɪs ˈmɔːnɪŋ. aɪ ˈwʌndər ɪf aɪ maɪt ˈkʌm ən ˈsiː jʊ tə ˈtɔːk tə jʊ əbaʊt ə ˈverɪ ɪmˈpɔːtənt ˈmætə.
- aɪm ˈrɑːðə ˈbɪzɪ ðɪs ˈmɔːnɪŋ. ˈkʊdənt jʊ ˈkʌm ðɪs ˌɑːftəˈnuːn?
- ət wɒt ˈtaɪm ʃəl aɪ ˈkʌm?
- ˈkʌm ət ˈfaɪv əˈklɒk.
- ɔːl ˈraɪt. aɪl ˈsiː jʊ ət ˈfaɪv. ˈθæŋk jʊ verɪ ˈmʌtʃ.
- ˈnɒt ət ˈɔːl.
- gʊdˈbaɪ, ˈpiːtə.
- gʊdˈbaɪ, ˈbɪl.

43
THE TIME

Clocks and watches are instruments for measuring and showing the time. They are very necessary in our daily life. We cannot live without them.

Do you know the difference between a watch and a clock?

A watch is a small clock which you can wear on your wrist or carry in your pocket. A clock is placed on the wall or on a table. There are also clocks which stand on the floor. We can see clocks on towers, like the famous Big Ben in London.

When we want to know the time we ask:

- What time is it? or
- What's the time?

Look at a clock. It has a face and two hands. The big hand points to the minutes and the little hand points to the hours.

Can you answer these questions?

- How many seconds are there in a minute?
- How many minutes are there in an hour?
- How many hours are there in a day?

clock reloj	**measure** medir	**the time** la hora
daily diaria	**minute** minuto	**tower** torre
face esfera	**point** señalar	**watch** reloj
hand manilla	**second** segundo	**wear** llevar puesto
hour hora	**show** mostrar	**wrist** muñeca

43

ðə 'taɪm

'klɒks ən 'wɒtʃɪz ər 'ɪnstrumənts fə 'meʒərɪŋ ən 'ʃəʊɪŋ ðə 'taɪm. ðeɪ ə 'verɪ 'nesəsərɪ ɪn aʊə 'deɪlɪ 'laɪf. wɪ 'kænɒt 'lɪv wɪ'ðaʊt ðəm.

du ju 'nəʊ ðə 'dɪfərəns bɪtwi:n ə 'wɒtʃ ənd ə 'klɒk?

ə 'wɒtʃ ɪz ə 'smɔ:l 'klɒk wɪtʃ ju kən 'weər ɒn jɔ: 'rɪst ɔ: 'kærɪ ɪn jɔ: 'pɒkɪt. ə 'klɒk ɪz 'pleɪst ɒn ðə 'wɔ:l ɔ:r ɒn ə 'teɪbl. ðər ər 'ɔ:lsəʊ 'klɒks wɪtʃ 'stænd ɒn ðə 'flɔ: - wɪ kən 'si: 'klɒks ɒn 'taʊəz, laɪk ðə 'feɪməs 'bɪg 'ben ɪn 'lʌndən.

wen wɪ 'wɒnt tə 'nəʊ ðə 'taɪm wɪ 'ɑ:sk :-

- wɒt 'taɪm ɪz ɪt? ɔ:r
- 'wɒts ðə 'taɪm?

'lʊk ət ə 'klɒk. ɪt hæz ə 'feɪs ən 'tu: 'hændz. ðə 'bɪg hænd 'pɔɪnts tə ðə 'mɪnɪts ən ðə 'lɪtl hænd 'pɔɪnts tə ðɪ 'aʊəz.

kən ju 'ɑ:nsə ði:z 'kwestʃənz?

- 'haʊ menɪ 'sekəndz ə ðər ɪn ə 'mɪnɪt?
- 'haʊ menɪ 'mɪnɪts ə ðər ɪn ən 'aʊə?
- 'haʊ menɪ 'aʊəz ə ðər ɪn ə 'deɪ?

44
TRAFFIC SIGNS

Mr Armstrong is teaching his pupils the Highway Code. He wants them to learn it well from the very beginning.

Mr Armstrong says:

Let's begin our lesson. First we must have a look at the traffic signs. After learning what they mean, you will be able to take your driving test. If you pass this test, you will be given a driving licence.

There are warning signs, which are mostly triangular, and signs giving orders, which are mostly circular. There are also information signs, which are rectangular.

Now, could you tell me the meaning of the following signs?

NO ENTRY
ROAD NARROWS
CROSSROADS
GIVE WAY
NO OVERTAKING
NO LEFT TURN
PEDESTRIAN CROSSING
AHEAD ONLY
DOUBLE BEND
TWO-WAY TRAFFIC

ahead todo recto
beginning comienzo
bend curva
driving licence carnet de conducir

driving test examen de conducir
meaning significado
narrow estrecharse
overtake adelantar

pass aprobar
pedestrian peatón
two-way doble sentido
very mismo
warning (de) aviso

The Highway Code El Código de la Circulación.

44
'træfɪk ˌsaɪnz

mɪstər 'ɑːmstrɒŋ ɪz 'tiːtʃɪŋ hɪz 'pjuːplz ðə ˌhaɪweɪ 'kəʊd.
hɪ 'wɒnts ðəm tə 'lɜːn ɪt 'wel frəm ðə 'verɪ bɪ'ɡɪnɪŋ.

mɪstər 'ɑːmstrɒŋ 'sez :-

'lets bɪ'ɡɪn aʊə 'lesən. 'fɜːst wɪ məs hæv ə 'lʊk 'ət ðə
'træfɪk ˌsaɪnz. ɑːftə 'lɜːnɪŋ wɒt ðeɪ 'miːn, ju wɪl bɪ
'eɪbl tə 'teɪk jɔː 'draɪvɪŋ ˌtest. ɪf ju 'pɑːs ðɪs 'test, ju wɪl bɪ
'ɡɪvən ə 'draɪvɪŋ ˌlaɪsəns.

ðər ə 'wɔːnɪŋ ˌsaɪnz, wɪtʃ ə 'məʊstlɪ traɪ'æŋɡjʊlə, ənd
'saɪnz 'ɡɪvɪŋ 'ɔːdəz, wɪtʃ ə 'məʊstlɪ 'sɜːkjʊlə. ðər ər 'ɔːlsəʊ
ˌɪnfə'meɪʃən ˌsaɪnz, wɪtʃ ə rek'tæŋɡjʊlə.

naʊ, kəd ju 'tel mɪ ðə 'miːnɪŋ əv ðə 'fɒləʊɪŋ 'saɪnz?

'nəʊ 'entrɪ
'rəʊd 'nærəʊz
'krɒsrəʊdz
'ɡɪv 'weɪ
'nəʊ ˌəʊvə'teɪkɪŋ
'nəʊ 'left 'tɜːn
pɪ'drestrɪən 'krɒsɪŋ
ə'hed 'əʊnlɪ
'dʌbl 'bend
'tuː weɪ 'træfɪk

91

45
A TRAIN JOURNEY

Jack and Sue are going to Birmingham to visit Sue's parents. It is eight o'clock in the morning and Sue is packing the cases. They have a lot of luggage to take with them.

The train leaves at half-past nine. At half-past eight, Jack calls a taxi. When the taxi arrives, he takes down all the cases. The taxi driver puts the cases in the boot of the car and on top.

Once in the station, Sue stays in the hall surrounded by the luggage, while Jack goes to the booking-office to get the tickets.

As their luggage is very heavy, Jack asks a porter to take it to the platform where the train is waiting. They get on the train, find their compartment, put all the cases on the rack and sit down to wait for the train to start.

Five minutes later, the train begins to move. First it goes through some tunnels. After that, all they can see are houses and factories. A few minutes later, they are out of the town and in the countryside.

As they have had no breakfast, Jack suggests going to the buffet car, which is four coaches along. After breakfast, they return to their compartment and sit down again. Jack takes out a newspaper and begins to read, while Sue looks out of the window at the landscape.

boot porta equipajes	**pack** hacer las maletas	**tunnel** túnel
landscape paisaje	**surrounded** rodeada	**wait** esperar
luggage equipaje	**top** parte de arriba	**while** mientras

45
ə 'treɪn dʒɜ:nɪ

'dʒæk ən 'su: ə 'gəʊɪŋ tə 'bɜ:mɪŋəm tə 'vɪzɪt 'su:z 'peərənts.
ɪt ɪz 'eɪt əklɒk ɪn ðə 'mɔ:nɪŋ ən 'su: ɪz 'pækɪŋ ðə 'keɪsɪz. ðeɪ
hæv ə 'lɒt əv 'lʌgɪdʒ tə 'teɪk wɪð ðəm.

ðə 'treɪn 'li:vz ət 'ha:fpa:st 'naɪn. ət 'ha:fpa:st 'eɪt, 'dʒæk
'kɔ:lz ə 'tæksɪ. wen ðə 'tæksɪ ə'raɪvz, hɪ 'teɪks daʊn 'ɔ:l ðə
'keɪsɪz. ðə 'tæksɪ ˌdraɪvə 'pʊts ðə 'keɪsɪz ɪn ðə 'bu:t əv ðə 'ka:
ənd ɒn 'tɒp.

'wʌns ɪn ðə 'steɪʃən, 'su: 'steɪz ɪn ðə 'hɔ:l sə'raʊndɪd baɪ ðə
'lʌgɪdʒ, waɪl 'dʒæk 'gəʊz tə ðə 'bʊkɪŋ ˌɒfɪs tə 'get ðə 'tɪkɪts.

əz ðeə 'lʌgɪdʒ ɪz 'verɪ 'hɒvɪ, 'dʒæk 'a:sks ə 'pɔ:tə tə 'teɪk ɪt
tə ðə 'plætfɔ:m weə ðə 'treɪn ɪz 'weɪtɪŋ. ðeɪ 'get ɒn ðə 'treɪn,
'faɪnd ðeə kəm'pa:tmənt, 'pʊt 'ɔ:l ðə 'keɪsɪz ɒn ðə 'ræk ən
'sɪt 'daʊn tə 'weɪt fə ðə 'treɪn tə 'sta:t.

'faɪv mɪnɪts 'leɪtə, ðə 'treɪn bɪ'gɪnz tə 'mu:v. 'fɜ:st ɪt 'gəʊz
θru: səm 'tʌnəlz. a:ftə 'ðæt, 'ɔ:l ðeɪ kən 'si: ə 'haʊzɪz ən
'fæktərɪz. ə 'fju: mɪnɪts 'leɪtə, ðeɪ ər 'aʊt əv ðə 'taʊn ənd ɪn
ðə 'kʌntrɪsaɪd.

əz ðeɪ həv hæd 'nəʊ 'brekfəst, 'dʒæk sə'dʒests 'gəʊɪŋ tə
ðə 'bʊfeɪ ka:, wɪtʃ ɪz 'fɔ: 'kəʊtʃɪz ə'lɒŋ. a:ftə 'brekfəst, ðeɪ
rɪ'tɜ:n tə ðeə kəm'pa:tmənt ən 'sɪt 'daʊn ə'geɪn. 'dʒæk 'teɪks
aʊt ə 'nju:sˌpeɪpə ən bɪ'gɪnz tə 'ri:d, waɪl 'su: 'lʊks aʊt əv ðə
'wɪndəʊ ət ðə 'lændskeɪp.

93

46
A VISIT

Margaret has come to visit her friend Anne Morton. They are now talking in the sitting-room. Anne's mother comes into the room. Margaret stands up and shakes hands with her.

- How are you, Mrs Morton?
- Fine, thank you, Margaret. I'm very pleased to see you. How's your mother? I haven't seen her for a long time.
- She's quite well, thank you.

Then Mrs Morton goes away and comes back with a trolley, where there is a teapot, three teacups, a dish with butter in it, a jar of jam, a plate with some slices of bread on it and a tin of biscuits. Mrs Morton serves tea, and they all have tea and eat bread and butter with jam and biscuits.

They talk for an hour about this and that. Suddenly, Margaret looks at her watch and says:
- Oh, it's very late. I must go back at once.

Mrs Morton and Anne accompany Margaret to the door.
- Goodbye, Mrs Morton. Good-bye, Anne.
- Goodbye, Margaret.
- Give my kind regards to your mother.
- Thank you, Mrs Morton.

jam mermelada
jar tarro
look at mirar

pleased contenta
stand up levantarse
talk hablar

teapot tetera
trolley carrito para servir

Shakes hands with her Le da la mano.
Give my kind regards to your mother Da recuerdos a tu madre.

94

46

ə 'vɪzɪt

'mɑːgərɪt həz 'kʌm tə 'vɪzɪt hə 'frend 'æn 'mɔːtən. ðeɪ ə 'naʊ 'tɔːkɪŋ ɪn ðə 'sɪtɪŋ‚rʊm. 'ænz 'mʌðə 'kʌmz ɪntə ðə 'rʊm. 'mɑːgərɪt 'stændz 'ʌp ənd 'ʃeɪks 'hændz wɪð hə.

- 'haʊ ə jʊ, mɪsɪz 'mɔːtən?
- 'faɪn, 'θæŋk jʊ, 'mɑːgərɪt. aɪm 'verɪ 'pliːzd tə 'siː jʊ. 'haʊz jɔː 'mʌðə? aɪ 'hævənt 'siːn hə fər ə 'lɒŋ 'taɪm.
- ʃiːz 'kwaɪt 'wel, 'θæŋk jʊ.

ðen mɪsɪz 'mɔːtən 'gəʊz ə'weɪ ən 'kʌmz 'bæk wɪð ə 'trɒlɪ, weə ðər ɪz ə 'tiːpɒt, 'θriː 'tiːkʌps, ə 'dɪʃ wɪð 'bʌtər ɪn ɪt, ə 'dʒɑːr əv 'dʒæm, ə 'pleɪt wɪð səm 'slaɪsɪz əv 'bred ɒn ɪt ənd ə 'tɪn əv 'bɪskɪts. mɪsɪz 'mɔːtən 'sɜːvz 'tiː, ən ðeɪ 'ɔːl hæv 'tiː ənd 'iːt 'bred ən 'bʌtə wɪð 'dʒæm ən 'bɪskɪts.

ðeɪ 'tɔːk fər ən 'aʊə əbaʊt 'ðɪs ən 'ðæt. 'sʌdənlɪ, 'mɑːgərɪt 'lʊks ət hə 'wɒtʃ ən 'sez :-
- 'əʊ, ɪts 'verɪ 'leɪt. aɪ məs 'gəʊ 'bæk ət 'wʌns.

mɪsɪz 'mɔːtən ənd 'æn ə'kʌmpənɪ 'mɑːgərɪt tə ðə 'dɔː -
- gʊd'baɪ, mɪsɪz 'mɔːtən. gʊd'baɪ, 'æn.
- gʊd'baɪ, 'mɑːgərɪt.
- 'gɪv maɪ 'kaɪnd rɪ'gɑːdz tə jɔː 'mʌðə.
- 'θæŋk jʊ, mɪsɪz 'mɔːtən.

47
THE WEATHER

In summer the sky is blue. In winter it is grey, as it is covered with clouds. In summer the sun shines and it is hot. Then we say that the weather is fine. In winter it often rains and it is cold. We say then that we have bad weather. When it is very cold, it snows.

Here is a conversation between an Englishman and a Spaniard:

- Look at the sky. It's grey.
- I think it's going to rain again.

At this moment it begins to drizzle and a few minutes later, it is raining hard.

- Look, it's pouring!
- Perhaps it's only a shower.
- I don't like English weather. I like the weather in my own country.
- What's the weather like in Spain?
- There's a lot of rain in the north of Spain, but it's sunny in the south. The sky is always blue there.
- What's the weather like in Madrid?
- In Madrid it's cold in winter and hot in summer.
- What about spring and autumn in Madrid?
- It's warm in spring and cool in autumn.
- Where are you from?
- I'm from Málaga. It's always spring there.
- No wonder you don't like English weather.

drizzle lloviznar   **pour** llover mucho   **shower** chaparrón
fine hermoso   **rain** lluvia, llover   **snow** nieve, nevar
hard intensamente   **shine** lucir, brillar   **sunny** soleado

47
ðə 'weðə

ɪn 'sʌmə ðə 'skaɪ ɪz 'blu: - ɪn 'wɪntə ɪt ɪz 'greɪ, əz ɪt ɪz 'kʌvəd
wɪð 'klaʊdz. ɪn 'sʌmə ðə 'sʌn 'ʃaɪnz ənd ɪt ɪz 'hɒt. ðen wɪ 'seɪ
ðət ðə 'weðər ɪz 'faɪn. ɪn 'wɪntə ɪt 'ɒfən 'reɪnz ənd ɪt ɪz 'kəʊld.
wɪ 'seɪ ðen ðət wɪ hæv 'bæd 'weðə. wen ɪt ɪz 'verɪ 'kəʊld, ɪt
'snəʊz.

'hɪər ɪz ə ˌkɒnvə'seɪʃən bɪtwi:n ən 'ɪŋglɪʃmən ənd ə
'spænɪəd :-
- 'lʊk ət ðə 'skaɪ. ɪts 'greɪ.
- aɪ 'θɪŋk ɪts gəʊɪŋ tə 'reɪn ə'geɪn.

ət ðɪs 'məʊmənt ɪt bɪ'gɪnz tə 'drɪzl ənd ə 'fju: mɪnɪts 'leɪtə,
ɪt ɪz 'reɪnɪŋ 'hɑ:d.
- 'lʊk, ɪts 'pɔ:rɪŋ!
- pə'hæps ɪts 'əʊnlɪ ə 'ʃaʊə.
- aɪ 'daʊnt laɪk 'ɪŋglɪʃ 'weðə. aɪ 'laɪk ðə 'weðə ɪn maɪ 'əʊn
'kʌntrɪ.
- 'wɒts ðə 'weðə laɪk ɪn 'speɪn?
- ðəz ə 'lɒt əv 'reɪn ɪn ðə 'nɔ:θ əv 'speɪn, bət ɪts 'sʌnɪ ɪn ðə
'saʊθ. ðə 'skaɪ ɪz 'ɔ:lweɪz 'blu: ðeə.
- 'wɒts ðə 'weðə laɪk ɪn mə'drɪd?
- ɪn mə'drɪd ɪts 'kəʊld ɪn 'wɪntə ən 'hɒt ɪn 'sʌmə.
- 'wɒt əbaʊt 'sprɪŋ ən 'ɔ:təm ɪn mə'drɪd?
- ɪts 'wɔ:m ɪn 'sprɪŋ ən 'ku:l ɪn 'ɔ:təm.
- 'weər ə jʊ 'frɒm?
- aɪm frəm 'malaga. ɪts 'ɔ:lweɪz 'sprɪŋ ðeə.
- 'nəʊ 'wʌndə jʊ 'daʊnt laɪk 'ɪŋglɪʃ 'weðə.

48
A WEDDING

John Taylor and Peggy Green are going to be married. The date is set. The wedding will take place on the 15th of June.

They are getting everything ready. They have sent invitations to all their friends and relatives, and now they are receiving a lot of presents.

* * * * *

The wedding day has arrived. Mr Thomas, a close friend of John's, will be the best man. This is the person that helps the bridegroom at the wedding.

Everything is ready. Mr Green, Peggy's father, is there to give away his daughter in marriage, and the priest is ready to celebrate the wedding ceremony.

Peggy, the bride, is wearing a white dress and she has a wedding-ring on her finger. Before the wedding, she wore only an engagement ring.

* * * * *

The ceremony is over and the guests are eating wedding-cake at the wedding reception.

After the reception, John and Peggy will go to the airport, as they intend to go to Rome for their honeymoon.

airport aeropuerto	**bridegroom** novio	**honeymoon** luna de miel
best man padrino	**daugther** hija	**set** fijada
bride novia	**engagement** compromiso	**wedding** boda

48

ə 'wedɪŋ

'dʒɒn 'teɪlə ən 'pegɪ 'gri:n ə 'gəʊɪŋ tə bɪ 'mærɪd. ðə 'deɪt ɪz 'set. ðə 'wedɪŋ wɪl 'teɪk 'pleɪs ɒn ðə 'fɪfti:nθ əv 'dʒu:n.

ðeɪ ə 'getɪŋ 'evrɪθɪŋ 'redɪ. ðeɪ həv 'sent ˌɪnvɪ'teɪʃənz tʊ 'ɔ:l ðeə 'frendz ən 'relətɪvz, ən 'naʊ ðeɪ ə rɪ'si:vɪŋ ə 'lɒt əv 'prezənts.

* * * * *

ðə 'wedɪŋ ˌdeɪ həz ə'raɪvd. mɪstə 'tɒməs, ə 'kləʊs 'frend əv 'dʒɒnz, wɪl bɪ ðə ˌbest 'mæn. 'ðɪs ɪz ðə 'pɜ:sən ðət 'helps ðə 'braɪdgrʊm ət ðə 'wedɪŋ.

'evrɪθɪŋ ɪz 'redɪ. mɪstə 'gri:n, 'pegɪz 'fɑ:ðə, ɪz 'ðeə tə 'gɪv əweɪ hɪz 'dɔ:tə ɪn 'mærɪdʒ, ən ðə 'pri:st ɪz 'redɪ tə 'selɪbreɪt ðə 'wedɪŋ ˌserɪmənɪ.

'pegɪ, ðə 'braɪd, ɪz 'weərɪŋ ə 'waɪt 'dres ən ʃɪ hæz ə 'wedɪŋˌrɪŋ ɒn hə 'fɪŋgə. bɪ'fɔ: ðə 'wedɪŋ, ʃɪ 'wɔ:r 'əʊnlɪ ən ɪŋ'geɪdʒmənt ˌrɪŋ.

* * * * *

ðə 'serɪmənɪ ɪz 'əʊvə ən ðə 'gests ər 'i:tɪŋ 'wedɪŋˌkeɪk ət ðə 'wedɪŋ rɪˌsepʃən.

ɑ:ftə ðə rɪ'sepʃən, 'dʒɒn ən 'pegɪ wɪl 'gəʊ tə ðɪ 'eəpɔ:t, əz ðeɪ ɪn'tənd tə 'gəʊ tə 'rəʊm fə ðeə 'hʌnɪmu:n.

99

49
THE WEEKEND

On Sunday mornings, people generally go to church, read the Sunday paper, have lunch and perhaps have a sleep afterwards.

In the afternoon, some people go to the cinema or to the house of some friends, where they play cards or have tea together. Other people prefer to stay at home reading a book, writing letters or watching television.

Some English people like working in the garden on Sunday afternoons. At night, they generally go to bed early because they have to get up early on Monday morning.

Some other people take advantage of having two days off to go to the country and breathe fresh air in order to escape from the noise and pollution of the town.

afterwards después	**escape** escapar	**people** gente, personas
air aire	**fresh** fresco	**pollution** contaminación
breathe respirar	**get up** levantarse	**sleep** siesta
church iglesia	**noise** ruido	**some** algunos, algunas
early temprano	**other** otros, otras	**together** juntos

Take advantage Aprovecharse.
In order to Con objeto de.
Two days off Dos días libres.

49
ðə ˌwiːkˈend

ɒn ˈsʌndɪ ˈmɔːnɪŋz, ˈpiːpl ˈdʒenərəlɪ ˈgəʊ tə ˈtʃɜːtʃ, ˈriːd ðə ˈsʌndɪ ˌpeɪpə, hæv ˈlʌntʃ ən pəˈhæps hæv ə ˈsliːp ˈɑːftəwədz.

in ðɪ ˌɑːftəˈnuːn, ˈsʌm ˈpiːpl ˈgəʊ tə ðə ˈsɪnəmə ɔː tə ðə ˈhaʊs əv səm ˈfrendz, weə ðeɪ ˈpleɪ ˈkɑːdz ɔː hæv ˈtiː təˈgeðə. ˈʌðə ˈpiːpl prɪˈfɜː tə ˈsteɪ ət ˈhəʊm ˈriːdɪŋ ə ˈbʊk, ˈraɪtɪŋ ˈletəz ɔː ˈwɒtʃɪŋ ˈtelɪˌvɪʒən.

ˈsʌm ˈɪŋglɪʃ ˈpiːpl laɪk ˈwɜːkɪŋ ɪn ðə ˈgɑːdən ɒn ˈsʌndɪ ˌɑːftəˈnuːnz. ət ˈnaɪt, ðeɪ ˈdʒenərəlɪ ˈgəʊ tə ˈbed ˈɜːlɪ bɪkɒz ðeɪ ˈhæv tə ˈget ˈʌp ˈɜːlɪ ɒn ˈmʌndɪ ˈmɔːnɪŋ.

ˈsʌm ˈʌðə ˈpiːpl ˈteɪk ədˈvɑːntɪdʒ əv ˈhævɪŋ ˈtuː deɪz ˈɒf tə ˈgəʊ tə ðə ˈkʌntrɪ ən ˈbriːð ˈfreʃ ˈeə ɪn ˈɔːdə tʊ ɪsˈkeɪp frəm ðə ˈnɔɪz ən ðə pəˈluːʃən əv ðə ˈtaʊn.

50
AT THE ZOO

A zoo is a park in which wild animals live in the open air.

The animals in a zoo cannot escape. Some live in cages and others, in enclosures.

Last Sunday, Mr Field decided to take all his family to the zoo for the day. As it is a long way from the place where they live, they took a bus there.

In the zoo they saw lions, tigers, bears, leopards, deer, monkeys, giraffes, camels and elephants.

There were people taking photographs, and Mr Field took some photographs of his children with the lions in the background.

They went to a very big pond, where there were some seals playing at catching fish that people threw to them.

At midday, the children were hungry and they ate some sandwiches at the snack bar in the zoo.

In the afternoon, they went to see the birds. The children laughed when they heard the funny parrots speak.

At about five, they caught the bus home.

background fondo	**funny** graciosos	**park** parque
bears osos	**giraffes** jirafas	**parrots** loros
birds pájaros	**heard** oían	**pond** estanque
cages jaulas	**laugh** reír(se)	**seals** focas
camels camellos	**leopards** leopardos	**speak** hablar
caught tomaron	**lions** leones	**threw** echaban
deer ciervo(s)	**midday** mediodía	**tigers** tigres
enclosures recintos	**monkeys** monos	**wild** salvajes

In the open air Al aire libre.

50
ət ðə 'zu:

ə 'zu: ɪz ə 'pɑːk ɪn wɪtʃ 'waɪld 'ænɪməlz 'lɪv ɪn ðɪ 'əʊpən 'eə.
ðɪ 'ænɪməlz ɪn ə 'zu: 'kænɒt ɪs'keɪp. 'sʌm 'lɪv ɪn 'keɪdʒɪz ənd
'ʌðəz, ɪn ɪn'kləʊʒəz.

'lɑːst 'sʌndɪ, mɪstə 'fiːld dɪ'saɪdɪd tə 'teɪk 'ɔːl hɪz 'fæmɪlɪ tə
ðə 'zu: fə ðə 'deɪ. əz ɪt ɪz ə 'lɒŋ 'weɪ frəm ðə 'pleɪs weə ðeɪ
'lɪv, ðeɪ 'tʊk ə 'bʌs ðeə.

ɪn ðə 'zu: ðeɪ 'sɔː 'laɪənz, 'taɪgəz, 'beəz, 'lepədz, 'dɪə,
'mʌŋkɪz, dʒɪ'rɑːfs, 'kæməlz ənd 'elɪfənts.

ðə wə 'piːpl 'teɪkɪŋ 'fəʊtəgrɑːfs, ən mɪstə 'fiːld 'tʊk səm
'fəʊtəgrɑːfs əv hɪz 'tʃɪldrən wɪð ðə 'laɪənz ɪn ðə 'bækgraʊnd.

ðeɪ 'went tʊ ə 'verɪ bɪg 'pɒnd, weə ðə wə səm 'siːlz 'pleɪɪŋ
ət 'kætʃɪŋ 'fɪʃ ðət 'piːpl 'θruː tə ðəm.

ət 'mɪddeɪ, ðə 'tʃɪldrən wə 'hʌŋgrɪ ən ðeɪ 'et səm 'sænwɪdʒɪz
ət ðə 'snæk bɑː ɪn ðə zu:.

ɪn ðɪ ˌɑːftə'nuːn, ðeɪ 'went tə 'siː ðə 'bɜːdz. ðə 'tʃɪldrən 'lɑːft
wen ðeɪ 'hɜːd ðə 'fʌnɪ 'pærəts 'spiːk.

ət əbaʊt 'faɪv, ðeɪ 'kɔːt ðə 'bʌs 'həʊm.

CONTENTS